Conspiracy Theories

Other books in this series by the same author

The Rise of New Labour
Who Shot JFK?

Conspiracy Theories

ROBIN RAMSAY

BARNES & NOBLE

NEW YORK

This 2006 edition published by Barnes & Noble, Inc. by arrangement with
Pocket Essentials.

ISBN-13: 978 0 7607 8715 1
ISBN-10: 0 7607 8715 8

A CIP catalogue record for this book is available from the Library of Congress.

Printed and bound in Spain

1   3   5   7   9   10   8   6   4   2

Contents

The World is Not Like That

The conspiracy theory boom of the last few years shows no sign of abating. Dan Brown's *The Da Vinci Code*, 20 million copies sold world-wide, which four million people have read in the UK, has ensured that. The fact that a *novel* about a conspiracy theory, involving a group which doesn't exist, could generate so much heat is another sign of conspiracy theories creeping into the mainstream. Even Polly Toynbee in *The Guardian* felt obliged to warn us of the pernicious nature of conspiracy theories. I agree with her: they are pernicious. Or, rather, to anticipate one of my arguments below, some of them are. The all-encompassing variety which offer to explain great chunks of history and politics by the secret machinations of small groups – the Jews, the Masons etc. – are pernicious. Before Dan Brown's naff novel it was the events of 9/11/2001 which gave birth to a great reef of theories in cyberspace; before that *The X-Files* in the mid 1990s boosted the number and visibility of conspiracy theories in popular culture. These are the major landmarks in the development of the 'conspiracy culture' and two of the three are fiction.

This 'culture's' distinguishing characteristic is the tendency to assume either that the deaths of all celebrities and all major geopolitical events are the result of conspiracies, or that all such events might be conspiracies.

Take the death of Princess Diana. The motives of those chiefly involved in the conspiracy theorising were mixed. The main impetus behind this undoubtedly came from Dodi Fayed's father, Mohammed El Fayed, and is perhaps understandable as the reaction of a grieving parent, with several hundred million pounds to spend, who has suddenly lost his son and his son's extremely glamorous girlfriend in a one-car crash. Encouraging Fayed's beliefs were some of the followers of Lyndon LaRouche Jr, a strange American conspiracy theorist whom I discuss below, who sees the evil hand of the British Royal family behind much of the world's troubles. For LaRouche's followers it is axiomatic that the British Royals killed Di. Conspiracy theorists seized on the words of Richard Tomlinson, the former MI6 officer who told the world of a British intelligence plan to kill the Serbian leader Slobodan Milosevic in a tunnel, using a bright light to disorientate the driver of his car. (One witness from Paris had reported seeing a flash just before Di's car crashed.) Recently the former MI5 officer Annie Machon has stated that she and her partner, David Shayler, suspect MI6's involvement (although they offer no evidence).[1] The driver of the car, Henri Paul, has been discovered to have received large amounts of unaccountable money and is suspected of being in the pay of MI6[2]; and the photographer James Andanson, the suspected driver of the white Fiat car, which was seen near the incident, has died a bizarre death.[3]

Although the major media are no longer pursuing the story, there are still many Internet sites discussing her death and the 'no conspiracy' verdict reached by the French legal inquiry and the 'no conspiracy' verdict we will undoubtedly get from the current, ongoing British police inquiry, will not deter the conspiracy theorists.[4] There are enough loose ends to keep the fire going.

Even the death of a relatively minor figure such as John F. Kennedy Jr in a plane crash in 1999 was immediately surrounded by question marks which ranged from the relatively simple – people reporting phenomena during the event not reported by the mass media – to full-blown conspiracy theories arguing that this latest dead Kennedy's alleged plans to run for President provided the reason for his assassination.

The stabbing of former Beatle, the late George Harrison, by a Beatles-obsessed mental patient, almost immediately, produced a preposterous piece of nonsense called 'Harrison Stabbing & Masonic Symbolism', which included the following:

> Considering...the Beatles' key, pivotal role in the mass social experimentation carried out by Britain's Tavistock Institute in conjunction with covert intelligence agencies like the CIA, NSA and Britain's MI5/MI6, we'd say there is a strong likelihood that Harrison, like Lennon, was NOT the victim of some random act of senseless violence...We'd say it's a good possibility Harrison was targeted to be bumped off by some of the same forces responsible for rubbing out Lennon, using MK-Ultra/Manchurian Candidate-type mind-controlled assassin Mark David Chapman.

I was more interested than I would normally have been in such twaddle because of the reference to the Tavistock

Institute in London. You cannot graze in the lush fields of American conspiracy theories for long before coming across the alleged role of the Tavistock Institute in the subversion of America in the 1960s but I had never understood what it was the Tavistock had done to deserve this reputation. The piece about Harrison gave me a clue, telling me:

> In fact, Lennon was murdered shortly after he gave an interview to *Playboy* magazine in which he blew the lid off the fact that the Beatles were part of massive experimentation in social control/engineering unleashed by Tavistock and intelligence agencies, as was the deliberate introduction of drugs like LSD into the burgeoning "counterculture" scene during the 1960s and 1970s. The *Playboy* interview was published not long after Lennon's death.

Just stop there and think about it. Had Lennon actually said any such thing it would have been a world-wide sensation. Since there was no such sensation, I knew without checking that John Lennon said no such thing. Nonetheless, I looked up the Lennon *Playboy* interview on the Net. I cannot pretend I read every word but, trust me, he does not mention the Tavistock Institute at all, let alone any of the rest of the nonsense attributed to him by our anonymous conspiracy theorist.[5]

The problem with the term conspiracy theory is that it comes with a lot of negative baggage. Some is recent, the accumulated effects of the mountains of ridiculous piffle on the Internet. Some of it is historical. To most of the intellectual Western world, to politicians, academics and journalists, and to most Marxists and socialists, 'a conspiracy theory' does *not* just mean a theory about a conspiracy but something much wider and more negative. At its worst 'conspiracy theory' evokes 'the conspiracy theory of history', the kind of all-encompassing conspiracy theory that argues that everything is the fault of, or everything is controlled by, X. In the past 300 years X has been, at various times, the Jews (or Jewish bankers), the Masons, the Catholics, the Communists, the Illuminati, or the Devil. More recently we have seen those conspiracy theories in which X is said to be the British Royal Family,[6] Aristotle Onassis,[7] the Committee of 300,[8] the alien-US military axis and shape-shifting, extraterrestrial alien reptiles.[9]

Such all-embracing conspiracy theories strike the orthodox, rational Western mind as absurd. We know that complex historical processes cannot be explained by the activities of some little group. The French and Russian revolutions, for example, cannot be explained by the existence of little cabals of Jewish bankers or Masons. The world is just not like that. Further, the term conspiracy theory was utterly *contaminated* by one such all-embracing conspiracy theory, the Jewish conspiracy theory, whose most enthusiastic adherents included one Adolf Hitler. At worst, describing someone as 'a conspiracy theorist' evokes the gas chambers and Hitler's insane obsession with the Jews.[10] The result has been a virtual prohibition on the use of the word 'conspiracy' in orthodox history or politics. For most of the chattering classes – the media and knowledge industry, academics, politicians and their assistants – to talk of conspiracy is to risk being called a conspiracy theorist; and to be so described is the kiss of death, the intellectual equivalent of being labelled a child molester.

Consequently, one of the bedrocks of the ideology of liberal democracies like ours is that conspiracy theories are always wrong, and that those who believe them are mental incompetents at best. This unquestioned belief manifests itself in sentences like, 'As usual the cock-up theory of politics turned out to be true'. Belief in the cock-up theory of history and politics is at the heart of what passes for political and intellectual sophistication in liberal democracies like ours. Public exposition of the cock-up theory of history shows that one is serious and aware of the inevitable and necessary complexity of the real world; and aware, too, of the inevitable incompetence of human beings. The subtext here is: only ignorant simpletons believe the world can be explained by conspiracies.

The proponents of the classic, all-embracing conspiracy theories – Nesta Webster,[11] the John Birch Society,[12] Gary Allen,[13] Lyndon LaRouche, the various neo-fascist and neo-nazi groups still clinging to the Jewish conspiracy theory and all the others – have indeed got it wrong but not because of their belief that small(ish) groups of people have had an influence on history. That is an unexceptional assumption. Small groups of people do indeed have an influence on history. Think of Lenin and the Bolsheviks or the financiers of the City of London or Bill Gates and his colleagues at Microsoft. It is false information and poor or non-existent attention to basic rules of evidence and inference which discredit the classic conspiracy theory.

For example, the belief that some Wall Street money ended up indirectly funding the Bolshevik revolution is a fundamental tenet of Gary Allen, the John Birch Society and other American right-wingers. It may be true. I have never tried to check this. Both the British and the then smaller US money markets had invested a lot of money in Russia in the 30 years before the Bolshevik coup of 1917. It would hardly be a surprise to find all the major money-lenders of Europe, a few of whom were Jews, in there, as well. (Money-lending was globalised then just as it is now.) When the German government funded Lenin's little group of exiled Russian revolutionaries during WW1 in the hope that they would take Russia out of the war and thus save Germany from fighting on two fronts, it is not inconceivable that some of the funds originally came from, say, loans made by non-German bankers, some of them Jewish. But some of the Americans who have found this important not only do not bother to check this factoid before recycling it, they further conclude, without evidence, that this proves that Wall St. was a bunch of Reds (or Jews, or Jewish Reds).

For example: it may be true that, as Nesta Webster believes, Masons had a part to play in both the American and French revolutions. There is some evidence for both propositions.[14] But Miss Webster did not actually offer much in her books, and this tells us nothing about the power of the Masons today – or in the 1920s, for that matter, in Webster's heyday.

For example: it clearly *is* true that the ramified Anglo-American network, centred round the Royal Institute of

International Affairs at Chatham House in Britain and the Council on Foreign Relations in America (discussed below), has had a considerable influence in shaping British and American foreign policy, especially before WW2. This is demonstrably true with or without Carroll Quigley's claims about the Round Table (discussed below). But this does not in any way substantiate the fantasies of the LaRouche organisation, which incorporated Quigley into an absurd (if entertaining) tale in which the UK controls America, the British Royal Family runs the world's drug traffic, organised the assassination of John Kennedy, etc etc.[15]

The aversion to talk of conspiracies on the part of the intellectually respectable is thus understandable up to a point. Who wants to be associated with the kind of rubbish propagated by people like LaRouche, let alone with people who think the world is being run by shape-shifting, extra-terrestrial lizards? However, this legitimate and under-standable allergy to mega conspiracy *theories* extends much further than the crazy fringe to a general prohibition on talk of conspiracy *per se*. Here is the American historian, Dr Jeffrey Bale, on the academic world's reactions to talk of conspiracy.

Very few notions generate as much intellectual resistance, hostility, and derision within academic circles as a belief in the historical importance or efficacy of political conspiracies. Even when this belief is expressed in a very cautious manner, limited to specific and restricted contexts, supported by reliable evidence, and hedged about with all sort of qualifications, it still manages to transcend the boundaries of acceptable discourse and violate unspoken academic taboos…The mere mention of the word 'conspiracy' seems to set off an internal alarm bell which causes scholars to close their minds in order to avoid cognitive dissonance and possible unpleasantness, since the popular image of conspiracy both fundamentally challenges the conception most educated, sophisticated people have about how the world operates, and reminds them of the horrible persecutions that absurd and unfounded conspiracy theories have precipitated or sustained in the past. So strong is this prejudice among academics that even when clear evidence of a plot is inadvertently discovered in the course of their own research, they frequently feel compelled, either out of a sense of embarrassment or a desire to defuse anticipated criticism, to preface their account of it by ostentatiously disclaiming a belief in conspiracies. They then often attempt to downplay the significance of the plotting they have uncovered. To do otherwise, that is to make a serious effort to incorporate the documented activities of conspiratorial groups into their general political or historical analyses, would force them to stretch their mental horizons beyond customary bounds and, not infrequently, delve even further into certain sordid and politically sensitive topics. Most academic researchers clearly prefer to ignore the implications of conspiratorial politics altogether rather than deal directly with such controversial matters.[16]

And the same processes occur within the world of politics and news gathering. I learned this first in 1986. At that time I was corresponding with Colin Wallace who was in Lewes prison. Wallace had worked for the British Army in Northern Ireland in the 1970s as an Information Officer and, later, as a psychological warfare officer. In the latter capacity he had become aware not only of various 'dirty tricks' being played in Northern Ireland, but also of the attempts by sections of the British secret state – notably MI5 – to smear the then Labour government of Harold Wilson. To discredit him, Wallace was framed for manslaughter and sentenced to ten years.

In late 1986, just before Wallace got out of prison, my then colleague in the magazine *Lobster*, Steve Dorril, and I had been trying to get the media interested in Wallace's story. We were invited to see some people at BBC's *Newsnight*. On informing Wallace of this, we were told that, among the visitors to his psychological warfare unit in Northern Ireland, known as Information Policy, had been Alan Protheroe. Twelve or thirteen years later in 1986, Alan Protheroe just happened to be Assistant Director General of the BBC. Nicknamed 'the Colonel' in the BBC, Protheroe was a part-time military intelligence officer, specialising in military-media relations. That the Assistant Director General of the BBC should be a state-employed, psy-war specialist in his spare time, with all that implies about contacts with the British military-intelligence complex…a blind man could have connected the dots. The point was that, unlike the journalists to whom we had been talking up to that point, who knew nothing of Wallace's career in Northern Ireland or of the activities of Information Policy, Protheroe knew who Wallace was and what the Information Policy unit had been doing. To the *Newsnight* journalists we therefore said something like this: 'Protheroe is a spook; you'll have to watch him. He will probably try to prevent the broadcast of anything about Wallace.' (A 'spook' is a loose description of someone who, while not an officer of an intelligence or security service, is linked with or works for one.) 'Really,' said the BBC people to whom we were we talking, 'it isn't like that in the BBC', and dismissed what we had said.

Subsequently a *Newsnight* journalist interviewed Wallace the day he came out of prison and then had his report yanked out of a programme at the very last minute. I was watching the programme and saw the confusion in the studio as the presenter tried to cope with the running order being re-jigged while they were on air. We subsequently heard that Protheroe had indeed blocked the Wallace interview but, when asked, the BBC denied that they had ever interviewed Wallace. Protheroe's action was confirmed four months later in the *Sunday Times* (5 April 1987), and has been acknowledged since by a senior *Newsnight* staffer who has now left the BBC. When the Wallace story reappeared again at the end of January 1990, the BBC used some of that 'non-existent' *Newsnight* footage to illustrate various news items about him.

The response of *Newsnight* people – 'it isn't like that at the BBC' – was comical, indeed preposterous. It was then only just over a year since there had been intense media interest in the revelation that the BBC actually had its own in-house MI5 office vetting BBC employees – *prima facie* evidence that the Corporation was exactly 'like that' on occasions. The *Newsnight* people did not say 'Protheroe isn't a spook' or 'We'll check it out' or even 'It sounds unlikely to us, but we'll bear that in mind'. All of these would have been rational responses. Instead, they dismissed what we had said out of hand because we were perceived to be offering them something from that most disreputable of categories, conspiracy theory.

But we had merely suggested three things:

1. Protheroe is a part-time intelligence officer.
2. In that role he knows what Wallace and Information Policy were doing.
3. Since Wallace's role and the work of Information Policy are still being denied by the British state, in our view it is probable that Protheroe will try to block transmission of Wallace's allegations.

Yet somehow these elementary and reasonable propositions triggered the 'Oh-dear-we-are-dealing-with-conspiracy-nutters' response, which turned their brains off.

It would be difficult to exaggerate how odd this utter aversion to talk of conspiracy is – especially on the part of journalists. It can hardly be disputed that, at any given time, there is an infinite number of political conspiracies, from the very small to the very large, which are going on in every industrialised society. Routine internal party politics, for example, is very largely conspiratorial, a network of interlocking cabals, plotting how to get their hands on this or that committee, group, district, meeting. Consider the example of the group of Labour MPs in 1980 who were planning to leave Labour and join the Social Democratic Party, then being created in secret. In the 1980 election for leader of the Labour Party there were two candidates: Michael Foot, the candidate of the left, and Denis Healey, the candidate of the right and centre. This group of Labour MPs, who were planning to leave Labour and join the Social Democratic Party because of Labour's alleged *left-wards* drift, voted for Michael Foot, the *left-wing* candidate, rather than Denis Healey. Their votes were enough to swing the leadership Foot's way. As one of them, Neville Sanderson, the source of this anecdote, said later: 'It was important that we finished off the job. It was very important that the Labour Party as it had become was destroyed.'[17] It was also revealed by Roy Hattersley that the notorious left-wing manifesto with which Labour went into the 1983 General Election (wryly described by Gerald Kaufman MP as the longest suicide note in history) was the result of a meeting to produce a manifesto at which the right of the party proposed nothing of their own and allowed the entire left agenda to go through unchallenged. The right had already decided Labour would lose the 1983 election and wanted the defeat to be laid entirely at the door of the left.[18] Thus the Labour Party's drift to the *left*, which, most political commentators agree, condemned it to the political wilderness from 1982 to 1997, was, in some part, the result of two conspiracies by *right-wing* members of the party.

At a less spectacular level, the 'pre-meeting meeting', before the group caucus, before the formal meeting, is, and always was, routine party politics. Both major political parties, at the parliamentary level, are divided into factions, some open, some not. For example, in the Tory Party of the 1980s, led by Margaret Thatcher, the most important faction was the 92 Group which, even after its existence had been reported in 1986, received hardly any attention from the media.[19] The 92 Group met in private and tried to influence political appointments and policies. In short, it was a political conspiracy but it was, of course, never called that. The 1999 book about the Labour Party's machinations in Wales by Paul Flynn MP is subtitled 'A New Labour Stitch-up'. The subtitle 'A New Labour Conspiracy' would have been much more accurate, for a conspiracy is what it was.[20] But 'stitch-up' sounds more harmless and does not place Flynn in the dreaded camp of those who believe in conspiracies.

Conspiracy is Normal Politics

The point I am probably labouring is that it is only a slight exaggeration to say, as the American writer and activist of the 1960s and 70s Carl Oglesby did, that conspiracy *is* normal politics carried out by normal means.[21] We could even extend his definition to include international relations and politics in which secret diplomacy and secret intelligence play major roles.[22] Yet this banal observation would simply be rejected – and probably laughed at as too ridiculous for consideration – by all mainstream political and intellectual circles in this country and the United States. Among 'the chattering classes', political sophistication demands the ritual trashing not only of the all-embracing conspiracy theorists, who deserve it, but virtually anyone who offers up a conspiracy of any kind.

The respectable Anglo-American 'chattering classes' reject all talk of conspiracy because (a) it conflicts with the model taught to them at university and (b) careers in British (or American) intellectual, political or media life are not aided by being identified with radical or deviant positions.

The hostility to conspiracies rests upon two false assumptions. The first is the juxtaposition of the complexity of social/political processes and the *presumed* simplicity of any explanation of events which has a conspiracy in it. This is false because, with the exception of small minorities who espouse the all-encompassing conspiracy theories, nobody is actually suggesting that complex social/political events can be explained by a single conspiracy. What might be called conspiracy *research* as opposed to conspiracy *theory* makes things *more*, not less, complex than the version served up by the respectable political classes. For example, the research into the conspiracy which killed John F. Kennedy has thus far generated hundreds of books, uncountable articles, half a dozen serious journals, millions of pages of declassified documents released by the US government and thousands of websites. [23]

The second false assumption is that there is always an either/or choice, either conspiracy or cock-up, when the real world is usually a complicated mixture of both. The Watergate affair, for example, contained a number of core conspiracies: the formation of the secret White House 'plumbers' covert action group, the plumbers' various illegal activities, including the break-in at the Democratic Party's office, and so on. But these were overlaid with the consequences of human error (cock-up), notably Nixon's White House recording system which recorded a number of incriminating conversations between Nixon and his aides. The Iran-Contra affair was triggered when a plane being used to transport secret supplies to the 'Contras' fighting the Nicaraguan government was shot down. One of the crew survived and, contrary to all good clandestine operational practice, he was carrying documentation which led investigators back to the White House and the hitherto secret operation – an illegal conspiracy – being run by a then unknown Colonel, Oliver North.[24] North's operation in the White House basement was then further revealed when investigators found hundreds of e-mail memos to and from his office which he thought he had destroyed when he pressed the 'delete' key on his computer.

The denouncing of 'the conspiracy theory of history/ politics', so commonplace among our respectable higher media, academics and politicians, is usually little more than the ritual thrashing of a straw-man almost entirely of their own construction. A more rational perspective takes it for granted that there are clandestine influences – conspiracies – at work in society. Not the ridiculous, world-controlling conspiracies involving the Masons, or the Illuminati, or Jewish bankers, or the alien 'greys', or other similar groups, but more mundane activities like intelligence agencies manipulating domestic and international politics, or companies buying government policies by making anonymous donations to political parties, or 'lobbying'.[25]

It became absurd to deny the existence of large-scale political conspiracies, or powerful 'hidden forces', as soon as the existence of the CIA or KGB – both vast state conspiracies – was revealed.

The irrationality of the all-embracing conspiracy theory is rightly contrasted with the rationality of the conventional view that things are complex. This is the concept of pluralism, the dominant political model in a liberal democracy like ours, our society's official picture of itself. Pluralism, as the term suggests, tells us that society is complex, that there are large numbers, a *plurality*, of groups and interests jostling for position and power: unions, owners of capital, political parties, lobby groups, trade associations, voluntary organisations, bankers, bureaucracies etc etc. This view is obviously true in general, but it tells us nothing beyond the general. What it does not tell us is which groups of the many that exist have the power – nor how they use it. The interesting questions begin where pluralism stops.

The concept of pluralism was popularised in the 1950s and used in the post-war struggle with the Soviet Union. They had dictatorship; we had democracy. They had the secret police; we had Parliament. Conspiracy was something the Reds did. This made a degree of intellectual sense in the first 25 years of the Cold War, when the existence of the Western democracies' own secret services was still more or less a secret. But it has made no sense for the last 25 years, when their existence has been revealed. In Britain, for example, among the many groups in our 'pluralist' society are state agencies – the armed forces, MI5, MI6,

Special Branches and GCHQ, for example – whose activities are not just largely secret but are intrinsically conspiratorial. The British state contains and is maintained by a group of official conspiracies about which the ordinary citizen is not allowed to know much. In the case of the intelligence, security and military services, the ordinary citizen is allowed to know virtually nothing. Studying the activities of organisations like the CIA or MI5 is not remotely similar to a belief in conspiracy theories about Jewish bankers or the Illuminati. The British author Anthony Summers put it very nicely when he said he was not interested in conspiracy theories but he *was* interested in theories about conspiracies.

Here is one of the American conspiracy world's more subtle commentators, the highly entertaining Robert Anton Wilson.[26]

'As Edward Luttwak documents in his cheerfully Machiavellian little text, *The Coup d'Etat*, more governments have been changed, since World War II, by the *coup d'etat* than by any other method. More governments have been changed by coup than by all the democratic elections and revolutions combined. Since every coup is by definition a conspiracy, this means that conspiracies have had more effect on the past 40 years of world history than all the electoral politics and all the popular revolutions added together. That is rather ominous, in a period when "educated" opinion holds that it is infamous, nutty, eccentric or downright paranoid to think about conspiracies at all. We are, in effect, forbidden to think about how the planet is actually governed.'[27]

Wilson is obviously exaggerating for rhetorical effect but his general point is well taken. The mysterious thing is not that some poor deluded fools insist on seeing conspiracies, but how it is that, for so long, so many apparently intelligent people – most Anglo-American political scientists and journalists, for example – have managed not to notice that conspiracy is an everyday, important part of the phenomena they purport to be studying and reporting. Let me give some more examples.

Since its formation in the 1920s until its demise about 15 years ago, an organisation called the Economic League collected and spent, in today's money, millions of pounds every year working against the British left. It produced propaganda, printed leaflets, planted newspaper articles, employed full-time speakers, ran courses and maintained a blacklist of 'subversives', access to which was given to employers who paid an annual subscription. It may have spent as much money as the Conservative Party since WW1. Yet there was not one academic essay on and virtually no journalistic investigation of the Economic League between its formation and 1988.[28] No history of British domestic politics in the twentieth century can be anything but incomplete without the Economic League, but I have never seen one that contains such an account.

Even more significantly, orthodox American contemporary history and politics somehow manages to skip over the fact that in a five-year period in the 1960s, one President, the probable next President and the most important black leader since WW2 were victims of assassinations which were never investigated properly and remain unsolved.

One of Those No-Weatherman-Required Situations

Britain was run for most of the twentieth century by two intensely secretive, overlapping groups. One is the British state, about which we know very little, thanks to this country's secretive culture. This is especially true of its secret branches about which even MPs are not allowed to ask questions. The other is the Conservative Party, about whose funding even its members know almost nothing.[29] In the USA since the Second World War, in the name of National Security and justified by the Cold War with the Soviet Union, a group of government military and intelligence agencies, headed by the CIA and the Pentagon together with their satellite supply companies (the military industrial complex, in short) has been operating, largely in secret and very profitably. It is frequently difficult to show the links between a society's dominant political ideas and the interests in it but, in these instances, it looks pretty straightforward. Some of the most powerful interests in Britain and the United States do not want their secret activities examined and it turns out that, in both societies, being interested in secret activities – in conspiracies – is intellectually disreputable and *verboten*.

Notes

1. See Annie Machon, *Spies, Lies and Whistleblowers* (Sussex: The Book Guild, 2005, pp. 212–216).
2. Paul had received £75,000 from the UK in the weeks before the accident. See <www.alfayed.com/details.asp?aid=150>

3. See Greg Swift, 'How did Diana paparazzo die?' in *The Daily Express*, 9 June, 2000. It is reproduced at <www.alfayed.com/details.asp?aid=57>

4. Google gave 34,000 hits for the request 'diana + conspiracies' in August 2005.

5. At <http://educate-yourself.org/nwo/nwotavistockbestkeptsecret.shtml> is a collection of nonsensical articles on Tavistock, with material like this in them:

> 'Today the Tavistock Institute operates a $6 billion a year network of foundations in the U.S., all of it funded by US taxpayers' money. Ten major institutions are under its direct control, with 400 subsidiaries, and 3000 other study groups and think tanks which originate many types of programs to increase the control of the World Order over the American people.'

The origins of this nonsense appear to lie in the role of some people associated with the Tavistock in WW2 black propaganda.

6. The views of the organisation headed by Lyndon LaRouche Jr. These are perhaps best expressed in the book by two of his followers, *Dope Inc.* There is a reasonable chapter on LaRouche in Jonathan Vanakin, *Conspiracies Cover-ups and Crimes* (New York: Dell, 1992: which has been reprinted and amended several times since then). The occasional LaRouchie I have encountered came across a bit like a paranoid, politicised – not unintelligent – evangelical Christian. The conversation proceeds fairly rationally up to a certain

point at which you can feel the steel shutters in their brains coming down. The LaRouche organisation is at

7. The so-called *Skeleton Key to the Gemstone File*. This has been the subject of two full-length studies and a collection of essays edited by Kenn Thomas and David Hatcher Childress, *Inside the Gemstone File* (Kempton, Illinois: Adventures Unlimited Press, USA, 1999). This writer published the first critique of *The Gemstone File* in *The International Times* in 1978. This is included in the Thomas/Childresss book. *The Gemstone File* is a strange mixture of facts and fantasies. Most of the key allegations are uncheckable; most that are checkable are false. Despite this it has now been circulating for over 25 years. The American writer Martin Cannon possesses some of the original letters by Bruce Roberts from which the Skeleton Key was extracted. He e-mailed me extracts in early 2000 and they show that Bruce Roberts was simply a schizophrenic.

8. The views of the British author John Coleman, now resident in the USA, who claims to be a former member of the British secret service, publishes a newsletter, *World in Review,* and is widely quoted in the conspiracy culture. Of his background I know nothing. Of his claims to have been a member of the Secret Intelligence Service I am profoundly skeptical but, since SIS does not publish a list of employees, past and present, I can only say that nothing of his that I have read has ever betrayed any sign of being the work of a former British intelligence officer.

9. The alien-government conspiracy nonsense is discussed in chapter 6. The shape-shifting reptiles theme comes from David Icke.

10. See *The History of an Obsession: German Judaeophobia and the Holocaust*, Klaus P. Fischer (London: Constable, 1998). This conflation of conspiracy theory with the Holocaust was illustrated when the *Washington Post* of 12 December 1999, commenting on the civil trial which concluded that James Earl Ray had not killed Dr Martin Luther King, said this:

> 'The deceit of history, whether it occurs in the context of Holocaust denial or in an effort to rewrite the story of Dr King's death, is a dangerous impulse for which those committed to reasoned debate and truth cannot sit still.'

Incidentally, given the role of the *Post* in not investigating – for example – the murder of Dr King, or even reporting the civil trial, the idea that it is committed to 'reasoned debate and truth' is self-delusory.

11. English author of the 1920s and 30s, discussed below.

12. On which see, for example, 'The John Birch Society', Allan Westin in *The Radical Right,* ed. Daniel Bell (New York: Doubleday, Anchor, 1964).

13. Co-author of one of the most influential of the John Birch books, *None Dare Call it Conspiracy*, (Seal Beach, California: Concord Press, many editions in the 70s). His co-author Larry Abraham wrote a much less well known sequel, *Call it Conspiracy* (Seattle: Double A Publications, 1985).

14. See J. M. Roberts, *The Mythology of the Secret Societies* (St. Albans: Paladin, 1972).

15. I first came across the LaRouche organisation in Bonn, Germany in 1979. They had a stall on the pavement selling LaRouche's books and magazines. The one that caught my eye, which I bought, had above the mast-head the slogan, 'End British Control of America'. More than twenty five years after the group's first appearance no one is sure what the group is doing or who – if anyone – is funding it.

16. Jeffrey M. Bale, '"Conspiracy theories" and Clandestine Politics' in *Lobster* 29. (See <www.lobster-magazine.co.uk>)The historian Thomas Mahl did his PhD on the British covert operations in the US between 1939 and the Japanese attack on Pearl Harbor, which were aimed against the isolationist politicians who opposed US entry into WW2. A fascinating thesis on a rarely-mentioned subject (British covert ops in the US), Mahl's thesis is very badly written. In 1998 his thesis was published as a book. Here is his reaction to an accusation that his work is conspiratorial.

> 'How does the historian avoid the charge that he is indulging in conspiracy history when he explores the activities of a thousand people, occupying two floors of Rockefeller Centre, in their efforts to involve the United States in a major war?'

From a review by Justin Raimondo of *Desperate Deception: British Covert Operations in the United States, 1939–1944* by Thomas F. Mahl, as published in the

December 1998 *Chronicles* issue (pp.24–6) and reproduced on A-albionic Research Weekly Update of 3 April
2000. <http://a-albionic.com/a-albionic. html>

So powerful is this refusal to believe that conspiracies exist, *The Spectator* (17 January 2004) felt it worth
publishing a piece by John Laughland entitled 'I believe
in conspiracies'. Citing Operation Northwoods, the
plans put to and rejected by the American Joint Chiefs
of Staff in 1962 to commit some terrorist acts such as
blowing up an airliner and blaming Cuba, and Iran
Contra, Laughland argued that political conspiracies
are real. His opening sentence was this masterpiece of
snobbery: 'Believing in conspiracy theories is rather
like having been to a grammar school: both are rather
socially awkward to admit.'

17. *The Sunday Telegraph* 14 January 1996.

18. Hattersley's comments in 'Comrades at War', part of
the series *The Witness Years*, BBC2, December 1995.

19. See 'Lost legions of the right' by Julian Critchley MP,
The Observer 10 August 1986. Even Critchley, a Tory
MP, was unsure of the 92 Group's origins, writing that
it 'was raised some years ago...'

20. Paul Flynn MP, *Dragons led by Poodles: the Inside Story of
a New Labour Stitch-up* (London: Politicos Publishing,
1999).

21. Oglesby is the author of one of the best books about
US conspiratorial politics, *The Yankee and Cowboy War:
Conspiracies from Dallas to Watergate and Beyond* (New
York: Berkeley Medallion Books, 1977).

22. A good illustration of this thesis is the history of post-

war Cyprus, Brendan O'Malley and Ian Craig's *The Cyprus Conspiracy* (London: I.B.Tauris, 1999), which describes a long succession of conspiracies by the US and UK governments in the post-war era to divide the Greek Cypriots from the Turkish Cypriots, prevent any 'Cypriot' identity developing which might demand the removal of the foreign bases on the island and so retain US and UK military and intelligence facilities there.

23. The recent book on post-war Cyprus, referred to in footnote 22, contains evidence of many interlocking, competing, overlapping conspiracies.

24. This is described in detail by one of the journalists who followed the story from this beginning, Robert Parry. See his *Lost History: Contras, Cocaine, the Press and 'Project Truth'* (Arlington [Virginia]: The Media Consortium,1999).

25. The day I was writing this paragraph *The Independent* carried yet another report on the affair of former German Chancellor Kohl and the secret funds he received from business sources and the French state.

26. From 'The Spaghetti Theory of Conspiracy', Robert Anton Wilson's introduction to Donald Holmes, *The Illuminati Conspiracy – The Sapien System* , MD(C)(1987) (New Falcon Publications, 655 East Thunderbird Phoenix, AZ 85022).

   Wilson was co-author of the fictional *Illuminatus Trilogy*, the first volume of which contained a very acute and funny parody of American mega-conspiracy theorists of the 1960s and 70s.

27. It says something about the wacky world of conspiracy theorists that some people ignored the fact that *The Illuminatus Trilogy* was fiction and claimed that Wilson and his co-author were telling the truth...disguised as fiction, of course.

28. The first academic writing on the League was Arthur McIvor, '"A Crusade for Capitalism": the Economic League, 1919–39' in *The Journal of Contemporary History*, Vol. 23, 1988. My comments about the academic historians applies equally to the British left. How could they expect to defeat an enemy about whom they knew so little?

29. The funding of the Conservative Party is another of those subjects which academic political scientists have managed *not* to study in the twentieth century. The first book on the subject was by a non-academic, Colin Challen, now a Labour MP. See his *Price of Power: the Secret Funding of the Tory Party* (London: Vision, 1998).

I Am Paranoid but Am I Paranoid Enough?

To the dismay of the intellectually orthodox, we are living through a veritable golden age – or nightmare age – of conspiracy theories, serious enough for the US State Department to issue a briefing against them.[1] Compare and contrast this situation with, say, 1963. Who was interested in conspiracy theories in 1963? In the UK, there was a handful of disgruntled racist Tories – the League of Empire Loyalists, for example, which became one of the foundation blocks of the National Front – and little groups of Hitler lovers clinging to the old Jewish banking world domination myth.[2] In the US, there was the John Birch Society, some other fringe far-right groups and a handful of Jew-haters and American Hitler freaks.[3] Conspiracy theories were out on the margin of the margins in 1963. These days we have got conspiracy theories everywhere, about almost everything; and belief in the existence of conspiracies has now penetrated large areas of popular American – and thus by import – British popular culture.

Conspiracies have been a staple of thrillers throughout the 20th century. Think of films by Alfred Hitchcock in the 1930s: *The 39 Steps*, *The Lady Vanishes*, *Foreign Correspondent*, for example, all feature conspiracies as their central theme. In the 1970s, however, the themes of conspiracy theories in mainstream popular culture began to change. Once the conspiracy had been by some external foreign power (Germany, usually, in the British versions, or Communist Russia) but, after Watergate, in American thrillers the 'threat', the 'conspiracy' became the American government or the state. For example, in *The Rock*, Sean Connery plays a British SAS officer who stole former FBI Chief J. Edgar Hoover's secret files in the 1960s and who has been illegally imprisoned ever since.[4] The final scene of the film shows the Connery character's sidekick, played by Nicholas Cage, picking up the files, hidden by Connery years before. As he and his girlfriend drive off Cage's character holds up a strip of microfilm and says to her, 'Want to know who really killed Kennedy?' *Conspiracy Theory* starred Mel Gibson as the victim of a US government mind control programme. For the first half of the film Gibson's character is portrayed as the demented, paranoid, conspiracy theorist so loved by orthodox academia and the media. In the second half his paranoia is shown to have a rational base. Oliver Stone's *JFK* presented one of the many conspiratorial versions of the JFK case in which the evildoers were government officials. And so on.

Most significant of all has been the popularity of the TV programme, *The X-Files,* whose thematic material was a compendium of American conspiracy theories of the previous two decades. With *The X-Files*, what had previously been in the background – or underground – suddenly appeared in the foreground. On the back of *The X-Files* a large media bubble was built in this country, at the height of which there were five professionally produced, full-colour, nationally distributed magazines (and one multipart work) devoted to the so-called '*X-Files* agenda' — in other words, to conspiracy theories and the paranormal.

Conspiracy theories have been in the mainstream for a while but, in early 2000, conspiracy theorists began getting onto mainstream television. Britain's Channel 4, for example, broadcast half a dozen programmes made by the website <disinfo.com> which carries a lot of conspiracy theories. Since then both the BBC and Channel 5 have made programmes about conspiracy theories.[5]

There are conspiracy theories in other countries. Antisemitic theories are all over the place, from the former Soviet Union and its empire (Solidarity in Poland in the 1980s was distinctly tinged by Jewish conspiracy theory) to the right of Japanese politics (even though there are no Jews in Japan). In France, Le Pen's National Front contains reminders of the Jew-haters of pre-WWII and the notorious Czarist forgery from the turn of the century, *The Protocols of the Learned Elders of Zion*, is still being distributed in the Arab world as if it was a real document which could explain the existence of Israel in its midst. In 2002 it formed the basis of a multipart TV series broadcast in Egypt.[6] No doubt, if I knew more languages, I would find conspiracy theories in all industrialised societies. However, in the UK, we are getting American conspiracy theories along with our American soap operas and fast food chains. The major exception to this is the Australian-based magazine *Nexus* which carries the *X-Files* agenda of the paranormal and conspiracy theories plus other examples of 'suppressed' or alternative knowledge in the fields of science, energy and health. (When I first saw *Nexus*, I assumed it was American and indeed, much of its contents are.)[7]

Most of the American conspiracy theories come from white people. There are some conspiracy theories in the Afro-American community. Some of the black American religious subcultures believed that Reagan had 666, the biblical mark of the beast, tattooed on the back of his skull, under his hair. Others have believed that the distribution of heroin among the black population was part of a plot by the government to keep black Americans down. A substantial percentage of African-Americans believed that the CIA was selling crack cocaine to help it finance the war against Nicaragua, after Congress cut off the funds for the war. This belief turned out to be half true. The CIA *was* allowing cocaine dealers to import cocaine in return for donations to the Contra war. A similar sort of theory is the idea that AIDS was a biological warfare experiment which escaped. A variation on this, enthusiastically propagated by the KGB's disinformation people, is the idea that AIDS was a germ warfare experiment designed by whites to kill blacks. Joshua Nkomo in Zimbabwe, whose son died of AIDS, expounded this thesis. In 1990 a survey was reported in the *New York Times* (29 October) which showed that 30% of Afro-Americans in New York City believed AIDS was an ethno-specific virus designed by the US military.[8] But American conspiracy theories – at any rate, the ones which get reported or get attention on the Net – seem to be primarily a white phenomenon; and primarily a white *male* phenomenon (although there are a few prominent women).[9]

Most people could produce a list of wacky conspiracy theories with very little research. Here are a few examples I came across, without looking for them, in a couple of months a few years ago. A number of books about the O. J. Simpson case appeared in the US after the trial. According to a contents summary I read in the catalogue of Tom Davis Books,[10] one such argues that the murders had their origins in the FBI blacklist of certain bar applicants (would-be lawyers) because of their antiwar activities. These unemployed lawyers assassinated Nicole Simpson and framed O. J. Simpson to compel the FBI to disclose the blacklist. Only in America, with one million lawyers, home of the lawyer joke, would someone imagine a murderous cabal of unemployed lawyers!

For a mere £95, somebody called Michael Todd, in Yorkshire, offered to provide evidence of a world-wide conspiracy called Operation PELT, with a secret HQ in Ireland and 30 offices world-wide. The aim of PELT, he claimed, is to destroy the entire alternative movement; health, green, eco etc. I wrote asking for a sample of his evidence but did not get a reply.

The administrator of the anti-fluoride organisation, the National Pure Water Association, wrote to me suggesting that the reason for the vilification of Yorkshire Water during the drought of 1995 was not Yorkshire Water's inability to provide water to all its customers, while paying its directors and shareholders large salaries and dividends, but their refusal to add fluoride to their water. She wrote: 'Much of the persecution of that company this year – leaks, dry reservoirs etc – is, *we are sure,* orchestrated "punishment" for their decision.' (my emphasis added) I wrote asking her for evidence, but received no reply.[11]

A UFO buff I know slightly tried to persuade me that the US has a secret base built under Loch Lomond in Scotland, from which mysterious craft emerge. (The UFO as underwater craft is one of the minor themes amongst UFO theories). Why, I asked, would they put such a base under the single most popular tourist spot on the west of Scotland, visited every day by hundreds, if not thousands, of people?

The difficulty – or the delight – in studying conspiracy theories is the fact that, buried in the stupid nonsense, there is often something of interest in almost all of these and similar subjects. A conspiracy of disgruntled unemployed lawyers seems an unlikely explanation of the O. J. Simpson case but, improbable though it sounds now, one day someone may show that OJ was framed (as the conspiracy theory believed by the majority of black Americans claims).

The anti-fluoride case, after years of being high on the crank list, is creeping into the mainstream. There are still water companies in the UK which are unable or unwilling to put fluoride in their water supplies because of local opposition. Even *Covert Action*, the very serious, American spy-watching journal, has published an article on the fluoride issue, Joel Griffiths' 'Fluoride: Commie Plot or Capitalist Ploy?' – something that would have been unimaginable a few years before when the fluoride issue was discussed almost exclusively by the far right.[12] The 'commie plot' in the title of Griffiths' paper refers to the belief, in some sections of the US far right in the 1950s and 1960s, that fluoridation was a communist conspiracy to pollute America's water. This was ridiculed in the Stanley Kubrick film *Dr Strangelove* in the portrait of the crazed US base commander, Jack D. Ripper (sic), played by the late, great Sterling Hayden, which probably put the anti-fluoride case back a generation in the process.

Good conspiracy theories never die: this is one of their defining features. No matter how stupid they are and how frequently they are refuted, they cannot be entirely destroyed. There is always another cohort of believers coming through to replace those who have abandoned the theory. On 29 June 1999 the Rumour Mills News Agency, carried on the *Konformist* Internet newswire, referred to a paper that was *allegedly* introduced in a Congressional hearing by a Russian defector. (It's getting flaky already...) This paper, purporting to be a Soviet report on the fluoridation of the American water supply, *allegedly* said that fluoride was known to cause neurological changes in the brains of children which would reduce their IQ. The paper supported a planned attack on America by fluoridating their water supply, thus reducing the intelligence level of Americans, and making a take-over of future generations of Americans much easier. So it was a commie plot after all![13] In fact, as Joel Griffiths' paper shows, the origins of the dumping of fluoride in drinking water lay in the desire of the US companies, who produced the otherwise useless and toxic fluoride as a by-product of other processes, to find a means of disposing of it. Dumping it in reservoirs was a terrific solution for them! There is a real case to answer from the anti-fluoride lobby, though it has yet to be taken seriously by the major media in this country or – oddly enough – by the growing consumer lobby concerned with the quality of the food we eat.

There surely is *not* a US base under Loch Lomond, and there surely is *not* a secret conspiracy between the alien 'greys' and the US government and there surely are *not* tens of thousands of Americans being kidnapped and sexually assaulted by aliens. But this does not mean that the *entire* UFO thing can be written off as nonsense, the phenomena explained away as hallucinations, weather balloons, experimental US aircraft or whatever. There are now too many videotapes of strange things in the sky to support the many reports of them from sensible, rational people. And how do we explain the fact that thousands of Americans – it is mostly Americans so far – have experienced and reported abduction by aliens? Whitley Streiber, author of *Communion*, describing his own encounters with aliens, reported in one of its sequels, *Confirmation,* that he received 30,000 letters, out of a total mailbag of 250,000, from people describing similar experiences. Since British Members of Parliament sit up and take notice if they get a couple of dozen letters on a subject, getting 30,000 letters on anything is absolutely mind-boggling. So is the fact that at least 30,000 people apparently have memories of something like, or reminiscent of, abduction by aliens. The alien abduction phenomenon is bizarre in the extreme and no one – certainly no one on the sceptical side of the argument – has come within shooting distance of providing an explanation of what is going on.

Behind a surprising number of the bizarre stories floating around in the cosmic conspiracy miasma there is something, however fragmentary, which is real. Sometimes even
the most implausible claim has to be taken seriously. Since
the early 1970s a handful of people had claimed that the US
never went to the moon. It was all faked in a movie studio,
they said, a large-scale piece of political propaganda in the
Cold War with the Soviet Union. The 1978 film *Capricorn
One*, with one O. J. Simpson among its cast, dealt with this
in fictional form – an early example of the post-Watergate
conspiracy climate being reflected in Hollywood. At first
glance this is profoundly implausible and stupid. A conspiracy that big would involve hundreds, maybe thousands,
of people keeping quiet for decades. It just could not be
done, could it? Even if you can envisage the American government's national security bureaucracy approving such a
high risk plan – and I cannot – it would be impossible to
keep secret. Somebody would talk or something would
leak or somebody would sell the story to the media for big
bucks.[14] But photographic experts now claim that some of
the photographs given out by NASA as shots of the moon
landings *were* done in a studio. There was a long, careful
and, I think, totally convincing analysis published in the
Fortean Times in January 1997. But even if true, what does
this suggest? Do fake pictures mean a fake moon-landing?
As a federally-funded bureaucracy, NASA's aim was to
achieve maximum publicity to enable it to extract maximum dollars out of Congress for future projects. It is more
likely, surely, that NASA just dummied up some photographs on earth. You get better pictures in a studio than on

the moon. In a studio, for example, you can spotlight the US flag on the otherwise rather dimly-lit lunar module. (And — who knows? — maybe the moon photographs wouldn't come out properly. Maybe they would get fogged as the lunar module passed through the Van Allen radiation belts around the earth.) And so, 25 years later, a photographer looks at these photographs and thinks, 'Hang on a minute. On the moon there is only one source of light. So where has the spotlight in this photograph come from?'

Over a decade ago, I met someone who believed that derogatory information about him was being inserted into novels and radio programmes. He pointed out paragraphs which he thought were aimed at him. The evidence was not convincing. There was nothing in the paragraphs that he pointed out to me. 'How is the material fed out to the writers?' I asked. 'That's obvious', he replied, 'through the publishers' secret society.' But, I pointed out, there was not a shred of evidence that such a society existed. In any case, he was manifesting all kinds of other symptoms of paranoia. He thought that all his phone calls were taped and that his house was bugged and so on. It was textbook paranoia. I concluded my visit by telling him that I thought he was crazy and should see a psychiatrist. Some months later he sent me a photocopy of an article containing the first exposé of a British publishers' secret society, of precisely the kind he had hypothesised.[15] I replied that this was definitely one up for him but I still did not believe his story. The fact that a secret society had been discovered inside the British publishing world did not make up for the fact that there was nothing in the books or in the radio programmes he had shown me that could reasonably be interpreted in the way he was doing so.

Paranoia and the Paranormal

Why there is a link between an interest in the paranormal, the occult and strange phenomena and an interest in conspiracy theories is unclear to me but it does exist. This connection is reflected in my own life. I was casually interested in the paranormal from the late 1960s after coming across a book in the public library about radionics and the 'black box', the object of much ridicule in those days, and I came across US conspiracy theories six years later. Even so I am unsure what the link means. Perhaps the best explanation is the most banal one. Perhaps if you are willing to believe that the orthodoxy is wrong in one area, the reality or non-reality of the paranormal, you are likely to consider that other orthodoxies could also be wrong. It may simply be down to personality types. However it is explained, interest in the two areas seems to have developed in parallel.[16]

In the UK, the landmarks on what might loosely be called the paranormal side of the agenda seem to me to have been the following. First came the book by Pauwels and Bergier, *The Dawn of Magic* (American title, *The Morning of the Magicians*), first published in the UK in 1963. It was Pauwels and Bergier who brought to a mass audience in Britain the subjects of psychic powers, apparent links between the occult and the Nazi regime in Germany, UFOs, strange anomalies in the natural world, theories about the pyramids and so forth.

Second was the series of books by the English writer John Michell, most famously *The Flying Saucer Vision* in 1967. This introduced ley lines, geomancy, numerology, and extraterrestrials – the whole of what is usually called 'earth mysteries'.[17]

The third landmark was the book *Psychic Discoveries Behind the Iron Curtain*, published by two *Reader's Digest* journalists in 1970, which showed that the Soviet Union's government was funding research into psychic and paranormal phenomena. This was enormously significant because, if a strictly materialist and anti-religious culture like the Soviet Union was taking the subject seriously, it was hard to argue, as most Western scientists then did, that this was all mystical nonsense.

Fourth was the emergence of Uri Geller and Matthew Manning in the mid 1970s – especially Geller, who appeared to demonstrate powers beyond the known laws of physics and was doing so to a large audience on television.[18]

The fifth significant feature was the work of people like Erich von Daniken who popularised much of this material with tales of strange phenomena – Bermuda Triangle, pyramids, Space Gods and so forth.

Sixth, throughout this period, in the background, was the UFO mystery which culminated in Spielberg's films *Close Encounters* in 1977 and then *ET*. *Close Encounters* was a brilliant evocation of the then dominant versions of the UFO contact story, which also incorporated material from other areas, such as the flight of US aeroplanes which apparently disappeared in 'the Bermuda triangle'.

And seventh was the explosion of UFO reports, stories of abductions, contacts, and landings by extraterrestrials which we received via the United States in the 1990s.[19]

This torrent of 'alternative' information[20] resulted in extraordinary publications such as the Frontiers Science catalogue which, in the days before the Internet, offered books or video tapes on Lost Civilisations – Mu, Atlantis, Lemuria – and a host of others in Africa, Central and South America.[21] It had material on cryptozoology (Big Foot, Sasquatch, Yeti) on giants and sea monsters, crop circles, Stonehenge and all the other stone architecture before Christ, extraterrestrial archaeology allegedly showing buildings on Mars and the Moon, antigravity devices, UFOs and aliens, free energy devices, Tesla technology; alternative science and treatments of every kind from cold fusion to radionics and Wilhelm Reich's orgone boxes, ley lines, earth mysteries, and geomancy. And it had a section called conspiracy and history.[22] It is this body of knowledge – let us call it 'knowledge' – which has provided the thematic background to *The X Files* and *Dark Skies* on TV and dozens of films coming across the Atlantic.

Notes

1. <http://usinfo.state.gov/media/Archive/2005/Jul/27-595713.html>
2. See, for example, *The British Political Fringe*, George Thayer (London: Anthony Blond, 1965).
3. See George Thayer, *The Farther Shore of Politics* (London: Allen Lane, The Penguin Press, 1968).

4. Hoover's secret files were also the subject matter of the best Robert Ludlum novel, *The Chancellor Manuscript* (1977).

5. This writer appeared in them.

6. The *Independent* 4 February 2000 reported that the Defence Ministry of the Syrian government 'runs its own publishing house that has printed an Arabic edition of that hoary old forgery, the Protocols of the Elders of Zion'.

7. Its UK edition is said to be selling over 20,000 copies. *Nexus* has a website at

8. There is a surprising (to me) amount of evidence to support this view – or what looks like evidence. This 'evidence' exists and continues to be advocated, chiefly on the Internet, even though former intelligence personnel from the Soviet bloc have admitted that they invented the story. This is discussed below in chapter 6.

9. I am not sure how this connects but there is a link here to the attitude of some feminists in the 1980s who saw investigative journalism – also heavily dominated by men – as 'stupid macho boys' games'.

10. One of the pioneers of mail order conspiracy books which seems to have gone out of business.

11. National Pure Water Association, 12 Dennington Lane, Crigglestone, Wakefield, WF4 3ET.

12. In *Covert Action Information Bulletin* no 42 (Fall 1992). An expansion of the same thesis is Christopher Bryson, *The Fluoride Deception* (New York: Seven Stories Press, 2004).

13. <www.rumormillnews.com> 29 June 1999. The column included this fairly typical piece of conspiracy theorist thinking.

> 'In the last week, I have read two websites that cover the physical illnesses that are caused by two different chemicals: Aspartame and Fluoride. *It is obvious to me* that the big chemical and pharmaceutical companies are engaging in a wholesale poisoning of the world to enhance their profits. (They may also be doing this to "dumb down" the people of the world so they can be easily subdued when the One World Totalitarian government kicks in)' (my emphasis added).

There are indeed considerable bodies of evidence which show that fluoride and aspartame are dangerous. But the connection made by the author – 'it is obvious to me' – exemplifies the causal jumps of conspiracy theorists' thinking.

14. The sharp-eyed reader will spot that this is precisely the line argued by the CIA against the Warren Commission critics in 1967, which I discuss below in chapter 4. In my defence I will merely comment that the Kennedy assassination could have been done – and in my view was done – by a handful of people: faking a moon shot could not.

15. Christopher Hurst, 'A touch of the leather aprons' in *The Bookseller,* 19 August 1988.

16. For example, I was twice invited to speak on conspiracy theories at the annual conference of the *Fortean Times*, this country's, and perhaps the world's, leading journal of strange phenomena. For Forteans,

conspiracy theories are another example of strange phenomena.

17. How far we've come since then is suggested by the appearance on Sunday, 23 March 1996 of an article in the *Sunday Telegraph* travel and tourism section on ley lines in England; or the wide acceptance today of feng shui, a domestic adaptation of geomancy. In 1966 there was not one book in print in the UK about ley lines and who had heard of feng shui?

18. On Geller see the very interesting biography, Jonathan Margolis, *Uri Geller: Magician or Mystic?* (London: Orion, 1998). Margolis began the book convinced that Geller was a fraud and ended up a believer. It is widely believed among the British media that in some way Geller has been exposed as a fraud by the Amazing Randi. As Margolis discovered, to his surprise, this is not so. There are obvious parallels with the story of Doug and Dave who claimed to have made some 'fake' crop circles. The fact that Doug and Dave could not possibly have made all the UK circles, let alone the circles appearing all over the world, meant nothing to the British mass media which chuckled, printed 'idiot circle believers hoaxed' stories, and consigned the subject to the dustbin. Meanwhile, without the assistance of Doug and Dave, crop circles go on appearing in the UK...

Matthew Manning these days seems to work solely as a healer but the book about his early life, *The Link* (New York: Holt, Rinehart and Winston, 1975) is worth getting from the library.

19. In the last few years it has been revealed that American as well as Soviet military and intelligence services have been examining many of these areas since the late 1960s – while routinely rubbishing other people who pursued them. See for example Jim Schnabel, *Remote Viewers: The Secret History of America's Psychic Spies* (New York: Dell, 1997) and Armen Victorian, *Mind Controllers* (London: Vision, 1998), chapters 9 and 10.

20. An acquaintance of mine reported that, in late 1999, in a branch of Waterstone's book shop in London the section headed 'Alternative History' was considerably bigger than the section just marked 'History'.

21. Without apparent anxiety it offered five conflicting identifications and locations for Atlantis, including one claiming that Atlantis was the state of Wisconsin in the USA!

22. But this catalogue – and others like it – was striking in what it did *not* offer to its readers. Its 'conspiracy and history' section included not one book by any of the serious American researchers of conspiracies, nor any of the many serious, well researched and documented books on the Kennedy assassination. The absence of the solid, academic work on the Kennedy assassination suggests that the conspiracy theory enthusiast does not want – or cannot handle – serious, well documented research.

From Blue Skies to Dark Skies

America – and, to a lesser extent, Britain – has been awash with conspiracy theories and the paranormal for the past decade or more. In the late 1990s some people attributed this to PMT – Pre-Millennial Tension. It is now clear that this was not a very significant factor. The millennium celebrations have been and gone and the conspiracy theories are still with us, although PMT added a peculiarly millennial flavour to some of the conspiracy theories emanating from the American Christian fringe.[1] The proliferation of conspiracy theories in the English-speaking world is attributable to more prosaic factors: the failing US empire, recent developments in technology, and the actual events in US political history since the sixties.

Although the triumphalist post-Cold War rhetoric may mask this, the American Dream is faltering. At best, real wage rates are no higher for many of the working class in America than they were twenty years ago. For some they are lower. The days when a middle class American family could afford to put their children through college on one (generally male) salary are over. The gap between the top income stratum in the US and the bottom is wider than it has been since the war, and getting wider every year. America, with 3% of the world's population, now has 25% of the world's prisoners in its booming prison system.[2]

Most of them are black and most of them are there for possession of drugs. The talk on the American left of an American prison *gulag* is not entirely specious. Things are not going according to plan for many of the white middle and working class Americans and they need to explain this to themselves.

Surveys regularly report that only around 2% of adult Americans read books of any kind. Most American newspapers and magazines barely mention the outside world, and the primary source of information for most Americans is television. But most American television simply does not deal with real political and economic issues in enough depth for the average American citizen to understand something as complicated as the economic decline of a great power. Faced as they are with anything from 30 to 120 cable TV channels putting out, at best, varieties of piffle, with tabloid comics like the *National Inquirer* (the forerunner of the British *Daily Sport*) and all its imitators in supermarkets putting out ludicrous inventions as 'news', is there any wonder that Mr and Mrs Joe Sixpack have trouble understanding the world and distinguishing between what is real and what is fake.[3] And the Sixpacks may have been 'born again'. By the standards of secular Britain, America is a profoundly religious society. People who believe in God and the Devil, who think that the bible is the literal account of the creation of the world,[4] do not have that far to go to believe that the sky at night is swarming with UFOs looking for people to abduct and experiment on; or that the United States government is about to surrender control of the US to the United Nations in the name of the New World Order; or that Bill Clinton's administration was preparing concentration camps to incarcerate 'the patriots' who might resist these changes.[5]

You can see the change of mood reflected in the US accounts of encounters with Extra Terrestrials. In the 1950s, when the US empire was booming, and the average white American consumer was experiencing continuously increasing material prosperity, the Extra Terrestrials reportedly meeting the America citizen, were largely benign,[6] making contact with the world to offer advice and friendship (and the occasional warning about the dangers of nuclear weapons). By the mid 1990s, with the US economic empire no longer delivering ever-increasing wealth for the vast majority of its white citizens, and with sections of the big American cities turning into facsimiles of the set of the film *Blade Runner*, the skies over America at night were apparently bustling with alien rapists, beaming down into people's bedrooms to scoop them up and take them away for extended sessions of sexual abuse, implantation of mind control devices and experiments. In the 1950s white America had blue skies. In the 1990s it had the TV series about the alien interaction with the earth, *Dark Skies*.

Many Americans perceive things going wrong – but not why. Not only are the information and the concepts they need not readily available, Americans are handicapped in their ability to understand the world by the power of the American myth. America is the country of manifest destiny, bearing the shining torch of freedom and democracy, the land of the free and the home of the brave. Most important and most inhibiting, America is a country whose official myth is that anyone can make it and become rich if they try hard enough. So deeply ingrained is this myth, many Americans simply find it impossible to believe that there is something wrong with their economic and social *system*. But if the *system* is fine, and things *are* going wrong, what is causing the problem? The answer is, of course, that things are going wrong because of the actions of...*bad people*. And they are doing it behind everybody's backs. This must be the case because most people cannot see them doing it!

The second factor in the rapid spread of conspiracy theories is technology. When I first became aware of US conspiracy theories in the late 1970s, the type-generating computer was not affordable, the fax machine had not been invented, photocopiers were expensive machines which still used rolls of coated paper and newspapers and magazines were still set in metal type. There were magazines discussing conspiracy theories – I remember one called *Conspiracy Digest* – but they were hard to find and had tiny circulations. Today, for a relatively small outlay, almost anybody can put their theories up on the Internet and wait for people to browse through them, pick them up and pass them on. Any old nonsense gets posted on the Net. There are no editors on your very own Web page, no demands for evidence.

However, by far the most significant factor in the recent rise of conspiracy *theories* is the existence of real conspiracies in US history. People believe conspiracy theories because they see a world full of conspiracies. Before the early 1960s, it was a variety of people on the far right who saw conspiracies to undermine America and to promote blacks, who believed in conspiracies by Jews, or bankers, or One Worlders. But American history since 1963 has provided *prima facie* evidence of political conspiracies:

- the assassinations of John and Robert Kennedy, Martin Luther King, many of the Black Panther leadership, Malcolm X and Jimmy Hoffa
- the shooting of Governor George Wallace when he appeared to threaten Richard Nixon's chances of winning the 1968 Presidential election
- the revelations in the 1960s of the various CIA operations run in the post-war years to influence world opinion
- the Vietnam War and the massive domestic surveillance and disruption programmes by the FBI and CIA run against the opponents of that war
- Watergate
- the revelation of CIA plots against foreign leaders in Watergate's aftermath
- the CIA shipping opium in Laos and Vietnam
- the revelation in the 1970s of the CIA's mind control programmes, MK-Ultra, Delta etc
- revelations of secret US government nuclear and medical experiments on its citizens

Since the advent of Republican governments in the 80s and the second Cold War, we have had Iran-Contra;[7] the October Surprise, the allegation that the Republicans did a deal with the Iranians holding American hostages to detain the hostages until after the 1980 American election, to prevent Democratic President Carter getting the electoral benefit of obtaining their release;[8] the clandestine arming of Iraq by Britain and America[9] and the subsequent operations to cover this up which, in Britain, involved major conspiracies to destroy companies and imprison witnesses;[10] billions of dollars ripped-off from the American Savings and Loan banks; hundreds of thousands of corpses in Central America – including a few American nuns and a local Archbishop – courtesy of death squad regimes working as US proxy governments;[11] and everybody and their cousin running cocaine into the US with the official permission of the CIA.[12]

We have had, in fact, what President Eisenhower warned America of in his farewell speech in 1960 – the military-industrial complex (with its intelligence agencies) running amok, totally beyond democratic control, gobbling up hundreds of billions of dollars. And we have had conspiracies, from every corner, day and night. The late Ralph J. Gleason's First Law of American Politics After Watergate conveys this shift: *no matter how paranoid you are what they are really doing is worse than you could possibly imagine.*

With Bill Clinton and the Democrats in office, the Republican Party and its allies on the right churned out conspiracy theories about Clinton. Some of these – those about his role, while he was governor of the state of Arkansas, in letting the CIA use facilities in Arkansas for the Contra war to run guns into Central America and cocaine back – seem to be true. At any rate, they are plausible and supported by evidence.[13] Many of the rest, the long lists of people alleged to have been killed covering-up this or that other conspiracy, the paranoia about Clinton trying to engineer an American Reich, suspending elections and putting the US under UN control, were dotty in the extreme.[14] Much of it was political pay-back, the right having their revenge for the long line of Republican disasters, beginning with Watergate and Nixon, which were exploited – however incompetently – by the Democrats. Some of it was simply psy-war aimed at discrediting Clinton and getting the Republicans back into office. Some of it, I would guess, was revenge by the US insurance companies whom Clinton had the temerity to challenge with his short-lived proposals for a system of government health insurance.[15]

Since Clinton we have had Bush, two stolen American Presidential elections, massive financial scandals (of which Enron and Worldcom are the best known) and the attack on Iraq prefaced by the fabrication of the intelligence on Iraqi weapons of mass destruction. And the commentators in the major media wonder why we believe in conspiracy theories?

Chris Carter, the writer/producer of the TV series, *The X-files*, has commented that his perception of the United States was formed by Watergate. But the key event was a decade before that – the killing of John F. Kennedy, and the refusal of a handful of stubborn Americans to accept the official government line that Lee Harvey Oswald did it. If any individuals are to be credited with starting the current mess we are in, it should be those critics of the Warren

Commission. Resisting all the government propaganda, the personal vilification and the manipulation by the media, they persisted and their persistence destroyed the government's case, and made the first big hole in the official, Disney version of America. From their research grew knowledge of the CIA and other US secret organisations and, without that knowledge, the US media would not have known enough to investigate Watergate and, from that point, to conduct more investigations of the CIA etc.

Fifty years of secrecy, lies, media manipulation and covert operations are coming back to bite the legs of the elite managers of American society and politics. The torrent of revelations since 1963 means that large numbers of US citizens no longer believe US government statements about *anything* and that a significant minority believe their federal government capable *of* anything, up to and including: planning to brainwash its citizenry (this is discussed below); detonating the bomb in Oklahoma to give itself a pretext for pushing draconian anti-terrorism laws through Congress; organising the plane-bombings of the Twin Towers on 9/11 as the pretext to invade Afghanistan and Iraq (discussed below); and even organising a secret conspiracy in the late 1940s with extra-terrestrial beings (discussed below).

So, why are we getting more conspiracy theories? It is at least partly the result of technology – computers and the Internet – and information overload, but the whole phenomenon is buttressed by what I'm still willing to call the *objective reality* of US politics and imperialism.[16] Twenty years after *Close Encounters of the Third Kind* and its still benign portrait of the human-extra terrestrial encounter, the makers of TV programmes like *The X-files* and *Dark Skies* took all the UFO material and added bits of everything else that was floating around on the fringes of science, mysticism and the paranormal. They then fused these with the conspiracy theory strand in post-1963 American politics to produce a series of overlapping paranoid nightmares. The paranormal-conspiratorial fusion on which such programmes are built has three elements:

1. An acceptance of what used to be described as the paranormal or psychic as real, routine and operational.
2. Distrust of any government, especially the US central government and a willingness to believe it capable of great evil and great secrecy – to believe, in short, that it is a conspiracy against its citizens.
3. The belief that there has been a massive US government cover-up of information on the subject of UFOs and that there has possibly been a cover-up of contact between extra-terrestrial beings and officials of the US government.

These elements were most comprehensively synthesised in the series *Dark Skies*, broadcast in this country on Channel Four in 1997, which rewrote some of the major events of US post-war history as if there really had been an on-going conspiracy between certain sections of the US government and aliens.

Notes

1. There are some examples in Kevin McClure's *Fortean Times Book of the Millennium* (London: John Brown Publishing,1996).
2. See *Guardian* 15 February 2000.
3. The claim that people are finding it harder to distinguish between fantasy and reality is difficult to sustain and is always pooh-poohed by the garbage media who claim that people know, for example, that the *Daily Sport* or the *National Inquirer* are not meant to be taken seriously. I am not so sure. The *Sunday Telegraph* some years ago carried a story about a policeman in London who was psychic. The policeman concerned was quoted as saying, 'At first my colleagues in the police force thought it was all a bit odd. But since the BBC programme *The X-Files*, many have given it a lot more credence.'

    But *The X-files* was fiction...
4. The teenage son of friends of mine began an Internet romance with an American girl. Eventually he went out to visit her in Kansas and was astonished to discover that in Kansas evolution is treated in the school system as of being no more intellectual value than so-called 'creation science'. This is now creeping into British schools thanks to New Labour's enthusiasm for 'faith schools'.
5. On American concentration camps see <http://www.apfn.org/apfn/camps.htm>
6. One of the minority of books reporting unfriendly

UFOs was Harold T. Wilkins, *Flying Saucers on the Attack* (New York: Ace Books, 1954).

7. See *The Iran Contra Connection: Secret Teams and Covert Operations in the Reagan Era* Peter Dale Scott, Jonathan Marshall and Jane Hunter (Boston: South End Press, 1987).

8. See Robert Parry, *Trick or Treason: the October Surprise Mystery* (New York, Sheridan Square Press, 1993). Parry runs the Media Consortium at <www.consortiumnews.com>

9. For an overall picture, see Kenneth R. Timmerman, *The Death Lobby: How the West Armed Iraq* (London: Fourth Estate, 1992). For the UK end, see John Sweeney, *Trading with the Enemy: Britain's Arming of Iraq* (London : Pan, 1993).

10. Chris Cowley, *Guns, Lies and Spies* (London: Hamish Hamilton, 1992), Gerald James, *In the Public Interest* (London: Little, Brown, 1995) and David Leigh, *Betrayed: the explosive questions the Scott Inquiry must answer* (London: Bloomsbury, 1993).

11. On Central America, William Blum's *Killing Hope: U.S. Military and CIA Interventions Since World War 2* (Monroe, Maine: Common Courage Press, 1995), is as good a place to start as any. Blum has a website at <http://www.killinghope.org> See also Robert Parry, *Lost History: Contras, cocaine, the press and 'Project Truth'* (Arlington: the Media Consortium, 1999).

12. See Peter Dale Scott and Jonathan Marshall, *Cocaine Politics: Drugs, Armies and the CIA in Central America* (Los Angeles: University of California Press, 1998). The

Agency admitted in 1998 that it had been given political permission in 1982 to ignore the drug dealing of
people working for the Contras – in effect a 'get out
of jail card' for any coke dealer willing to give a few
thousand dollars to the Contras. See 'CIA turned a
blind eye to Contras drug smuggling' in *The
Independent* 7 November 1998. This uncomfortable
fact has been largely ignored by the major American
media – apparently because they had spent so long
denying it to be true!

13. See, for example, Terry Reed and John Cummings,
Compromised: Clinton, Bush and the CIA, (Penmanin
Books [USA] 1995, ISBN 1883955025). There is also
pretty substantial but not conclusive evidence that
Clinton, while a Rhodes Scholar at Oxford University,
had been recruited by the CIA to report on American
students in the UK who opposed the war in Vietnam.

14. For example, one of many, the 1994 'Murder, Bank
Fraud, Drugs and Sex' by Nick Guarino, editor of *The
Wall Street Underground,* which alleges 21 murders by
the Clinton circle. On the phenomenon of the anti-
Clinton stories being generated on the right, see
Robert Parry, 'Dark smears of a mean machine' in the
Guardian 4 August 1994. One of Clinton's aides,
Sydney Blumenthal, described the anti-Clinton cam-
paign in some detail in his 2003 memoir *The Clinton
Wars (*London: Viking, 2003).

15. *Flashpoint, A Newsletter Ministry of Texe Marrs*, June 1995,
has as its page 1 headline, 'Fascist Terror Stalking
America'. Marrs state: 'The destruction of the

Reichstag in Berlin and the federal building in Oklahoma followed similar patterns. Both Hitler and Clinton cynically used the tragedies to justify Gestapo campaigns against their enemies...an evil clique of un-American money-hungry greedsters and murderers has grabbed the reins of such powerful groups as the CIA, FBI, DIA, DEA, DOD and BATF...' Published by Living Truth Ministries, Austin, Texas. Love the bit about 'un-American money-hungry greedsters'...

16. The idea that since the Republicans are saying it about a Democratic President it must be false, has undoubtedly contributed to the American liberal-left's inability see what Bill Clinton actually is – the mouthpiece for the American global corporations whose members sponsored him in the Trilateral Commission. This is discussed in Chapter 4.

I Can't See Them But I Know They are There

The most durable of the all-embracing conspiracy theories is the anti-Jewish one. Although the persecution of Jews can be traced back to the Middle Ages, the starting point for the contemporary conspiracy theory scene is the famous forgery by the Czarist secret police, *The Protocols of the Learned Elders of Zion*. This preposterous forgery has been in circulation for nearly a century.[1] (It is a measure of the *need* racists have to hate somebody that they ever took this baloney seriously.) The *Protocols* was a particular spin on an established tradition, which explains political and social change by the activities of secret groups of conspirators. In this instance, it was overlaid with hatred of Jews. That secret societies were believed to be powerful in 19th century Europe is not surprising. Most regimes were, or had recently been, monarchies and most monarchies were run and policed by little groups of people around the King or Queen who faced constant opposition and plotting by rival groups. The ruling elites of 19th century Europe also had experience of secret societies of working men (forerunners of trade unions), of masons and so on. Threats to the established order were associated by the powers-that-be with secret societies. The memory of the guillotine was still fresh in the collective mind of Europe's rulers.

After the 1917 Russian Revolution, the Jewish and Masonic fantasies of the 19th century merged with the fear of Bolshevism in post-World War I Europe and two different strands emerged. One was the 'Communism is Jewish' belief which survives, in little pockets, on the far right today; the other was the influential synthesis by the British writer, Nesta Webster, who detected the hand of an 18th century Masonic lodge, the Illuminati, behind both French and Russian revolutions.[2]

While Webster's theory had a brief vogue in Britain in the 1920s – even Winston Churchill seems to have swallowed it, briefly – it really took root in the United States, notably with the John Birch Society. The Birchers moved from a mainline, albeit extreme, anti-communist viewpoint in the early 1950s, via Carroll Quigley's account of the Round Table network (discussed below), to a muddled view in which the Illuminati have a definite, although vague, role to play.[3]

The John Birch Society, and similar, smaller groups on the American far right, incorporated the 19th century belief in the threat of secret societies, the 'isolationist' beliefs of the 1930s that the US ought not to get embroiled in the evil, decadent ways of Europe, the anti-communism which was the official ideology of the Western world for half a century; and fragments of real information about the elite planning bodies of Anglo-American (and later European and Japanese) capital. At its least rational this kind of thinking comes out as great dollops of fudge. In the 1950s one account of the supposed enemies the Society faced described them as a 'Fabian, Rhodes Scholar, Zionist, Pinko,

Communist, New Deal, Fair Deal, Socialist-minded gang'.[4] By 1997, when the Birchers had subsumed the Illuminati and the group of theories which go under the heading of 'the New World Order' into their world view, this had become 'the Illuminati's Socialist/Communist/Freemasonic New World Order'.[5] As new information comes along it gets added on the top, like layers of sediment.

This loosely assembled conspiracy theory received a massive boost with the publication in 1966 of Carroll Quigley's famous book *Tragedy and Hope* which revealed the existence of the Round Table network, set up with Cecil Rhodes' money just before and just after WWI.[6] The revelation of this network, and especially of its links to its US branch, the Council on Foreign Relations (CFR), seemed to offer the proof required of the great conspiracy – if not quite the conspiracy the US radical right was expecting. For while the radical right was aware of the CFR and the Rhodes Scholar programme, they had not connected them. Quigley seemed to join up the dots.

For noticing the significance of Quigley's book when the establishment had closed ranks to freeze it out,[7] we owe thanks to the radical right. For Quigley is the starting point for the examination of the influence of elite groups on Anglo-American-European history. The sequence of events is this. In the beginning (1908–1920) Cecil Rhodes' money created the Round Table groups in the British Commonwealth, the Royal Institute for International Affairs (Chatham House) in London, the Council for Foreign Relations (CFR) in the US, and the various branches of the

Institute of Pacific Affairs. Quigley does not actually provide the evidence for these claims but even a casual skim through the conventional literature on the period shows that they are basically correct.[8] These events took place when Britain was still – just – top dog in the world and this network of what would now be called think tanks and political action groups tried to formulate and implement foreign policies which would (a) benefit Britain and America and (b) move the world in the direction Rhodes sought, towards an Anglo-American dominated commonwealth of nations. (The term commonwealth came from the Round Table people.)[9]

By the end of WWII, when the US had supplanted the UK as the world's leading imperial power, the British dominance of this network was over. During the war the Council on Foreign Relations (CFR) planned the expansion of the US empire in the post-war years without discussing it with its UK counterpart. Although allies with Britain in the war against the Axis powers, elements of American business and the government spent the war planning how to get their hands on the British Empire after it.[10]

The CFR *has* dominated the ranks of the US foreign service for most of the post-war period. On that the US 'radical right', the elite conspiracy theorists, are correct. Virtually all the foreign policy managers of America in the post-war world have been members of the CFR.[11] But it is not clear to me that this tells us anything, any more than the fact that their UK equivalents, almost without exception, will have attended Oxford or Cambridge University.

In the early post-war years other groups of elite managers were formed. One was the Bilderberg group, begun in 1954 by the Polish *eminence grise* Joseph Retinger, working for the British MI6, and funded by the CIA. For almost 30 years Bilderberg was simply not reported on by the major Anglo-American media. One British journalist, Gordon Tether, who tried to write about the group in his column in the *Financial Times*, had those columns pulled from the paper, eventually lost his job after 20 years at the FT, and ended up publishing the columns which the FT had refused to print, including three on Bilderberg, in a little pamphlet.[12]

Although the major media on both sides of the Atlantic have continued by and large to accept the Bilderberg's requests for secrecy, the group has been reported on in the USA in a magazine called *The Spotlight* for over a decade.[13] In the current climate of slightly greater openness, one of Bilderberg's guests, Tony Blair, belatedly included his visit to a Bilderberg conference in his Parliamentary declaration of interests but only after an initial parliamentary answer denying that he had attended the meeting. Asked by the Conservative MP Christopher Gill which members of his government had attended meetings of the Bilderberg Group, Blair – or his office – replied in a written answer on 16 March 1998, 'None'. In fact, as well as Blair, Gordon Brown, Peter Mandelson and George Robertson from New Labour had attended Bilderberg meetings. Even more interestingly, I was informed by Bilderberg's administrator that the late John Smith, leader of the Labour Party before Tony Blair, was on the Bilderberg Steering Group from

1989 to 1992. Smith's role in the inner councils of Bilderberg sits uneasily with the public image of Smith as the genial, honest, Scots, 'old Labour' lawyer.[14]

In the last couple of years, apparently in response to stories about the group on the Net, Bilderberg has ceased to be quite as secretive as it used to be and a couple of major British newspapers, the *Mail on Sunday* and *The Scotsman*, have published pieces about the group. In late 1999, for the first time in the group's existence, the minutes of that year's meeting were leaked, extracts were published in the magazine *The Big Issue*, and the whole document was posted on the Internet.[15] This remarkable event was not recorded by any of the mainstream British media. It was apparently not a story.[16]

As the post-war capitalist world changed, notably with the emergence of Japan as a major economic power, members of the American Council on Foreign Relations formed the Trilateral Commission in the 1970s, consisting of representatives of the United States, Europe and, for the first time, Japan.[17]

Why the Right?

The role of elite management groups, such as the Trilateral Commission and Bilderberg Group, is one of the strands in the otherwise wacky world of contemporary conspiracy theory worth taking seriously and it is now, almost exclusively, highlighted by the radical right. This was not always the case. When Jimmy Carter, hitherto an obscure southern governor, appeared as a front-runner in the race for the

1976 US presidency, sections of the American left became interested in the role of the Trilateral Commission of which he had been a member. This brief flurry of interest led to the 1980 book *Trilateralism,* still the best single volume on the elite management groups.[18]

Bill Clinton was also another obscure southern governor until being adopted by the Trilateral Commission. Is this a coincidence? No, it is not. For the Democratic Party has a recurring problem when it comes to finding a plausible presidential candidate. The coalition of groups which elects a Democrat president includes the so-called Dixiecrats, white Democrats in the southern states. To get their votes *and* the votes of the black Americans of the northern cities is a neat trick. Hence the recurring appeal of televisual, southern Democratic governors – good old boys – to the corporate leaders of America. One of the roles of the Trilateral Commission in the United States – like the Bilderberg Group in Europe – is to assess politicians and promote those deemed acceptable by the corporate managers.

The strange truth about all this is that the Anglo-American left is basically not interested in these elite management or power elite groups. Despite the groups being composed entirely of the major figures from world capital and politics – the left's supposed enemy – somehow the left found this of little interest. Apart from that brief flutter of interest in the late 1970s when Trilateralist Jimmy Carter became president of the US, the Anglo-American left has passed on these groups, leaving them to the right.

Why it has happened that it is chiefly the right which is

interested in large scale conspiracies in general, and these elite groups in particular, is not clear. In part, the left's focus on systems rather than people – crudely, capital rather than capitalists – led it not to pay attention to the details. In part, it is the result of the subject of the elite management groups becoming 'contaminated' for those on the left by the interest in it expressed by the far right.[19] In other words, such is the left's fear of being linked with the right, anything the right takes up immediately becomes 'untouchable' to the left.

The radical right has two distinct views:

1. There is what we might call the hard-core view that hidden forces are running the world – the classic all-encompassing conspiracy theories. False though most of the popular versions of this are, it is not possible simply to say they will *always* be false. There *are* powerful secret or semi-secret societies in the contemporary world: think, for example, of the Masons (especially the Italian version, P2), Opus Dei, and the Knights of Malta.[20] Recently there has been interest in the Yale University-based secret society, Skull and Bones.[21] In Britain the Masons have local influence in certain sections of society, notably the police and local government.[22] In Italy, P2 even acquired national power for a while.[23] And if we did not know about P2 in the 1970s, what is its equivalent today of which we are as yet unaware?

2. The soft-core view of the right goes something like this. There are transnational forces which are seeking to undermine the nation state and/or the status quo. This *is*

correct, to an extent. There are indeed globalising forces trying to diminish the nation state. The world capitalist system is regulated – in theory, anyway – by institutions: the International Monetary Fund, the World Bank and the World Trade Organisation, which are dominated by Americans, and which represent the interests of the big corporations, most of them American. Transnational corporations do not like nation states because nation states are among the few organisations capable of opposing them. The policies of organisations like the IMF or World Trade Organisation *are* formulated, in part, at gatherings of the world's elite such as Bilderberg and the Trilateral Commission.[24] But, having correctly identified them as significant, the right has fundamentally misinterpreted these elite discussion groups as the master controllers – the executive committees, the boards of directors – of the capitalist universe, bent on subjugating the entire globe to their plans for a New World Order.[25] The evidence suggests that the CFR, Bilderberg, Trilateral etc. do not, in fact, pull the levers but merely set agendas and try to produce a consensus. At least the right, however, takes these groups seriously. The transatlantic left – and the major media – mostly ignores them.

The EU

Let us take the European Union as an example of the influence of the elite groups. Romano Prodi, President of the European Commission in the late 1990s, was a Steering

Committee member of the Bilderberg Group in the 80s. Prodi has limited the declarations of interests required of his Commissioners to the last ten years, something not done in the previous Commission, and so has avoided declaring his Bilderberg role in the 1980s.

Prodi's 20 Commissioners include seven other identified members of the elite management groups:

- Mario Monti, Steering Committee member of Bilderberg ('83–'93), member of the Executive committee of the Trilateral Commission Europe, from 1988 to 1997
- Pedro Solbes Mira, Trilateral Commission since 1996, Bilderberg 1999
- Chris Patten, Trilateral Commission
- Gunther Verheugen, Bilderberg 1995
- Antonio Vitorino, Bilderberg 1996
- Erikki Liikanen, Bilderberg 1999
- Frits Bolkestein, Member of the Royal Institute of International Affairs, Chatham House, in London; Bilderberg 1996[26]

From its inception, the European Union was the creation of political and business elites and the notional bits of democracy – the talking-shop parliament and elections to it – were added later.[27] The late Hugo Young's history of Britain's relationship with the EEC/European Union[28] describes in great detail the conspiracy by a section of the British state to get Britain into the EEC/EU. Young seemed to think he had diminished or made ironic the conspiratorial aspects of this with his book's title, *This Blessed Plot*. In fact, using the most official of sources – the hitherto secret Foreign Office account of the negotiations with the EEC/EU – he describes a conspiracy by a group of politicians and officials, led by the Foreign Office, to deceive the British people. Everything, and more, the British Eurosceptics have claimed for the last 25 years is confirmed.

Uncle Sam Needs Us

The European Movement was one of the organisations funded by the CIA in the 1950s in Uncle Sam's search for reliable anti-Soviet alliances.[29] The Cold War was fought largely as a series of clandestine conspiracies by both sides. Each reported to its populace the conspiracies of its opponents but not its own. American and British attempts to penetrate Soviet airspace on intelligence missions led to shooting encounters, which were never reported in Britain or America, in which hundreds of people died.[30] In the 1950s, the Americans made attempts to control a huge chunk of the non-communist world. By the mid-1950s they had made major inroads into Western European trade unions[31] and the CIA was running a massive propaganda operation, centred round the organisation called the Congress for Cultural Freedom.[32]

Other programmes existed to influence public opinion in Britain. Sympathetic Brits visited America on schemes that included Harkness, Fulbright and Kennedy scholarships; various Congressional programmes; the Smith-Mundt scholarships; Eisenhower Exchange Fellowships; and the State Department's Young Leader programme (so wide-ranging that, at different times, it embraced both Roy Hattersley and Margaret Thatcher). In 1983, newly elected MP Tony Blair took the American freebie trip.

Another set of organisations have promoted the Anglo-American alliance: the British Atlantic Committee, the Atlantic Council, the British North-American Committee, the British Atlantic Group of Young Politicians, the Atlantic Education Trust, the Atlantic Information Centre for Teachers, the Standing Conference of Atlantic Organisations, the Trade Union Committee for European and Transatlantic Understanding, and many others. These Anglo-American bodies presumably have counterparts in all the other NATO countries as well as other countries with which the US is allied, although I know of no system-atic research on them. Generally such bodies are only visi-ble to the public during periods of crisis. When the New Zealand government in the early 1980s tried to enforce a 'no nuclear ships' policy on the US Navy, the New Zealand-America network suddenly became newsworthy to the New Zealand media, as the US began leaning on the Kiwi government.[33]

Of organisations of this type, the one currently most of interest in Britain is the Trade Union Committee for European and Transatlantic Understanding (TUCETU). This began as the Labour Committee on Transatlantic Understanding in the 1970s, and was founded by Joseph Godson, Labour Attaché at the US embassy in London in the 1950s, who talent-spotted and promoted among the

British labour movement. Organised by two officials of the NATO-financed Atlantic Council, TUCETU incorporated Peace through NATO, the group central to Conservative Defence Secretary Michael Heseltine's Ministry of Defence campaign against CND in the early 1980s. It receives over £100,000 a year from the Foreign Office. TUCETU chair Alan Lee Williams was a Labour defence minister in the Callaghan Government before he defected to the SDP; director Peter Robinson runs the National Union of Teachers' education centre at Stoke Rochford near Grantham. In the mid-1980s Williams and Robinson were members of the European policy group of the Washington Centre for Strategic and International Studies.

The Atlantic Council/TUCETU network provided New Labour's first Ministry of Defence team. The initial Defence Secretary, George Robertson, now head of NATO, was a member of the Council of the Atlantic Committee from 1979–90; Lord Gilbert, Minister of State for Defence Procurement, is listed as TUCETU vice chair; and MoD press office biographical notes on junior Defence Minister John Speller stated that he 'has been a long-standing member of the Trade Union Committee for European and Transatlantic Understanding'.[34]

BAP

The latest in the long line of American-funded groups seeking to keep the British ruling elite pro-American began life as the British American Project for the Successor Generation and is now known just as the British-American

Project, or BAP for short. You may not have heard about BAP because the major media in Britain have mostly ignored it, in the same way they mostly ignore the Ditchley Foundation,[35] the CFR, Bilderberg and the Trilateral Commission. But BAP organises large annual gatherings, runs UK and US offices and publishes a newsletter, albeit one to which you and I cannot subscribe. In this newsletter BAP members are kept up to date about the career developments of other BAP members. The BAP newsletter's message is clear enough: stick with us, boys and girls, and you will go far. After the 1997 British general election the BAP newsletter headline was 'Big Swing to BAP' as it celebrated the arrival of five BAP alumni in the Labour government: namely the late Marjorie Mowlam, Chris Smith, Peter Mandelson (now an EU Commissioner), George Robertson (now Secretary General of NATO) and Elizabeth Symons (a junior Foreign Minister in the House of Lords). Other senior Labour figures to have been involved with BAP are Jonathan Powell, Blair's chief of staff, Geoff Mulgan, until recently a member of the Downing Street Policy Unit and Matthew Taylor, some time Head of Policy at Labour Party HQ.[36]

The BAP is interesting but not exceptional, nor, probably, particularly influential. These groups are *not* primarily interested in conspiratorial manipulation of policy but in maintaining the Atlanticist view, the kind of instinctive pro-American, pro-NATO consensus which is so powerful in this country that as soon as anyone strays from it in, say, a *Newsnight* interview, Jeremy Paxman's eyebrow rises and his voice gives the viewers the cue that, no, this person is not to be taken seriously. (Paxman, coincidentally, has been on a BAP jamboree.)

Like the Round Table, the Council on Foreign Relations, Ditchley, Wilton Park,[37] and Chatham House, the BAP is not so much a secret organisation, as a discreet organisation. This tradition of discreet, publicity-averse, elite gatherings will continue so long as the British and American elites find them useful ways of agreeing an agenda, building networks and getting their views across without the impedence of the electorate and democracy. Equally such groupings will continue to be the subject of conspiracy-theorising as long as they continue to look like conspiracies. And they will continue to look like conspiracies as long as the rest of us are kept in the dark about their activities.

The Official Conspiracy Theory

It was the powers-that-be in 19th century Europe who were first attracted to ideas of conspiracy to explain the uprising of their citizens against them. To some extent the survival of the all-encompassing conspiracy theory into the 21st century is simply an historical anachronism. But the survival of such theories has certainly been assisted by almost a century of official propaganda by the Western states about the reality of a vast Soviet conspiracy. Once that was believed, the right did not find it so hard to accept the reality of other conspiracies. From 1918 until the fall of the Soviet empire in 1989–91 we have all been officially encouraged to believe in the existence of the red menace. In post-WWII Britain the most important and successful conspiracy theorists were the cold warriors who pumped out endless stories of Soviet espionage and subversion in this country since the war. These reached some kind of climax in the 1974–77 period when a number of large-scale disinformation projects were mounted by the Anglo-American intelligence services against the labour movement, the Labour Party and Harold Wilson in particular, claiming that the Red Menace was taking over Britain.

Mrs Thatcher was one of those who believed the cold warriors' tales of the Soviet menace in Britain. She looked at the Trades Union Congress and saw Moscow subversion – 'the enemy within'. On the basis of nothing more than the fact that Labour Prime Minister Harold Wilson made a number of visits to the Soviet Union during the Cold War, Mrs Thatcher, like many others in her circle on the right of the Tory Party at the time, suspected that Harold Wilson was a KGB agent. They believed this strongly enough to voice it to a very senior civil servant in the administration of Wilson's successor, James Callaghan.[38] After becoming leader of the Tory Party in the mid 1970s, she was tutored in her belief in the reality of the Soviet 'threat' by a group of cold warriors, including perhaps the most important of them all, Brian Crozier.[39] Crozier had worked for much of the post-war period for the CIA and a British state propaganda and disinformation organisation called the Information Research Department (IRD) whose chief function was to propagate the official Communist conspiracy theory.[40]

To ensure that we believed in the reality of this approved conspiracy theory, the Anglo-American intelligence services – outstanding examples of institutionalised conspiracies in the 20th century – have spent large sums of our money propagating it while simultaneously denigrating anybody who proposed any other kind of conspiracy theory. This hypocrisy reached some kind of peak in 1967 when the CIA – a vast world-wide conspiracy – put out a message about the Kennedy assassination to all its stations and personnel. By 1967 the first wave of critics of the Warren Commission, notably Mark Lane and Edward Epstein, had appeared and were getting attention, especially abroad. The instruction from CIA HQ in Langley, Virginia, was that CIA personnel were to use their political and media assets to propagate the idea that the kind of conspiracy described by the Warren Commission critics could not possibly exist.

Three years before this comic event, the CIA's formal relationship with the Warren Commission investigating JFK's assassination was handled by the late James Jesus Angleton, head of CIA counter-intelligence, even though – or, perhaps, because – Angleton's department was deeply embroiled in the mysterious goings-on in Mexico City, into which Lee Harvey Oswald had wandered.[41] Having been conned by his friend, Kim Philby, and aware, via the Venona decrypts of Soviet wartime radio communications, of the scale of Soviet espionage in America during the war,[42] Angleton became increasingly, and many would say disablingly, paranoid. Angleton believed, among other things, that the split between the Soviet and Chinese Communist Parties in the 1960s (up to and including a shooting war on their borders) was a disinformation campaign to lull the

West into a false sense of security.[43] There are people on the fringe on the UK-US intelligence services who believed for years after the fall of the Soviet empire that the whole thing – demolishing the Berlin Wall, reuniting Germany and all – was a deception operation. *That's* a conspiracy theory worthy of the name!

Notes

1. The Protocols have been debunked many times. I have a 1938 version, John Gwyer, *Portraits of Mean Men: A Short History of the 'Protocols of the Elders of Zion'*, (Bristol: Cobden-Sanderson,1938). The standard text is Norman Cohn, *Warrant for Genocide: the myth of the Jewish world conspiracy and the Protocols of the Elders of Zion*, (Harmondsworth: Penguin,1967).

2. On Nesta Webster see Richard Gilman, *Behind World Revolution: the Strange Career of Nesta H. Webster*, (Ann Arbor: Insight Books, 1982). Roberts, see note 14 chapter 1, discusses the little that is known about the Illuminati. Despite the absence of evidence for the Illuminati's existence beyond about 1790, the group continues to haunt the imaginations of some people. The Christian Science University – apparently a breakaway from the official Christian Science organisation in the United States – reported in April 2000, in an 'Alert' on its Website, <www.tscu.org>, that 'A diabolical and Satanic legal scheme has been designed and is being prepared for global implementation by anti-Christ agents of an organisation called "The Illuminati"

Thanks to Tony Hollick for the TCSU reference.

3. See for example Gary Allen and Larry Abraham's *None Dare Call it Conspiracy* and Abraham's update *Call It Conspiracy*, both cited in note 13 to chapter 1. Abraham can't quite shake the old Illuminati habit and quotes (p. 257) the Illuminati's alleged founder Weishaupt, and states, 'Weishaupt's strategy still holds'. Which is a long way from saying the Illuminati are the conspiracy behind the conspiracies.

4. Cited on p.77 of George Thayer, *The Farther Shore of Politics* (London: Allen Lane/Penguin, 1968). Though the John Birch Society's influence has declined since its peak in the early 1960s it is still going. It has a website at <www.thenewamerican.com>

5. Description in a 1997 US newsletter from evangelical Christian David Smith of Waxahachie, Texas.

6. Macmillan (US) 1966 originally but now republished by several organisations on the US right. To my knowledge Quigley was discussed first outside the far right in this country in Robert Eringer, *The Global Manipulators* (Bristol: Pentacle, 1980).

7. It seems to have attracted only two tiny reviews in the *Virginia Quarterly Review*, Spring 1966, and *Annals of the American Academy of Political and Social Science*, November 1966.

8. I discussed this in a piece in *Lobster* 1, which I reprinted in number 25 with the arrival of Bill Clinton as a president who spoke publicly of his admiration for Quigley, one of his tutors at university. His comments about Quigley generated delirious fantasies on the far

right but – alas? – it was clear from those comments that Clinton had never come across Quigley's two books on the 20th century ruling elites and was not, as the far right hoped, acknowledging his (Clinton's) role as the stooge of the Round Table-Fabian-One World conspiracy!

9. Rhodes actually dreamed of reuniting Britain and its former colony, America, and one of the Americans in the Round Table network, Clarence Streit, argued the case for this in *Union Now* (London: Right Book Club, 1939) and *Union Now With Britain* (London: Jonathan Cape, 1941). This idea still has echoes today in the idea, current in some sections of the anti-EU Conservative Party and some areas of the City of London, that Britain should join up with the US in a North American Free Trade Area, rather than proceed further into a federal European Union.

10. See Laurence H. Shoup and William Minter, *Imperial Brain Trust* (London and New York, Monthly Review Press,1977) for an account of the wartime planning for the post-war era by study groups set up by the Council on Foreign Relations.

11. See for example <www.geocities.com/CapitolHill/2807>

12. C. Gordon Tether, *The Banned Articles of C. Gordon Tether* (ISBN 00905821009).

13. *The Spotlight* documents the US-dominated elite groups like Bilderberg while offering its readers the anti-Jewish conspiracy theory it detects beneath the New World Order.

14. In 1992 he became leader of the Labour Party.
15. *The Scotsman* 11 May 1998, *Mail on Sunday* (Night and Day section) 14 June 1998. Best single article on the Bilderbergers is Mike Peters, 'Bilderberg and the origins of the EU' in *Lobster* 32 (December 1996). This is among the material on the Bilderberg at Tony Gosling's site <www.bilderberg.org/>. The first book published in this country, outside the far right, to discuss the group was Robert Eringer's *The Global Manipulators* – see note 6 above. On the far right it was the subject of a chapter in National Front founder A. K. Chesterton's *The New Unhappy Lords*, (Hampshire: Candour Publishing, UK, 4th edition, 1975).

    The 1999 Bilderberg minutes are (as of August 2005) on Tony Gosling's site <http://www.bilderberg.org/>

16. My suspicion would be that self-censorship rather than censorship is the order of the day. Why write a story in which you know your editor is not going to be interested?

17. The Trilateral Commission's website is at

    On the history of the organisation – and more on the Bilderberg group – see Holly Sklar (ed.) *Trilateralism*,(Boston: South End Press, 1980). Among the Trilateral Commission's members in the early 1970s was the then young, largely unknown, Governor of Georgia, Jimmy Carter. Among the Trilateral Commission members in the 1980s was the then largely unknown, young Governor of Arkansas, William Jefferson Clinton.

18. Edited by Holly Sklar, this was subtitled *The Trilateral Commission and Elite Planning for World Management*. Though written from a left perspective, it has mostly been bought by people on the American right.

19. The idea of ideological or political 'contamination' was first expressed by Mike Peters in his essay 'Bilderberg and the origins of the EU' in *Lobster* 32. This is on the Web at

20. An early example of an attempt to deal rationally with this fuzzy area is in Jonathan Marshall's essay 'Brief notes on the political importance of secret societies' originally published in Marshall's short-lived *Parapolitics USA* and republished in *Lobster* issues 5 and 6, 1984.

21. Kris Mulligan (ed.) *Fleshing out Skull and Bones* (Waterville, Oregon: TrineDay, 2003) contains a great deal of information on Skull and Bones members plus a lot of conspiratorial nonsense. It doesn't seem clear to me that Skull and Bones is a secret organisation. Any visitor to Yale University can see the Skull and Bones headquarters in a large building in the centre of the campus.

22. See Martin Short, *Inside the Brotherhood* (London: Grafton Books, 1989), for many British examples.

23. On P2 see Philip Willan, *Puppet Masters: The Political Use of Terrorism in Italy* (London: Constable, 1991).

24. On the Trilateral Commission, see Stephen Gill, *American Hegemony and the Trilateral Commission*

(Cambridge: Cambridge University Press, 1990).

25. These ideas, now widespread on the US populist and Christian right, have penetrated as far as former Republican Presidential candidate, the Reverend Pat Robertson. Robertson's 1991 book articulating some of this was the subject of two long articles expressing shock and incredulity at this fact in the *New York Review of Books*, 2 February 1995 and 20 April 1995.

26. This section on the elite affiliations of EU commissioners is a summary of an article in *Lobster* 38. Most of the information on the affiliations of the Commissioners came from their declarations of interest.

27. There are now said to be 10,000 lobbyists in Brussels working the European Commission and Parliament. See *Europe Inc*, Balanya, Doherty, Hoedeman, Man'anit and Wesselius, (London: Pluto, 2000) p. 3. This book is the work of Corporate European Observatory and much of the material here is at their site <www. xs4all.nl/~ceo/>. This is the place to start in understanding the nature of the EU.

28. *This Blessed Plot* (London: Macmillan, 1998).

29. See Richard Aldrich, *The Hidden Hand: Britain, America and Cold War Secret Intelligence* (London: John Murray, 2001) ch. 16.

30. See Paul Lashmar, *Spy Flights of the Cold War* (Stroud, Glos.: Sutton, 1996).

31. This subject has yet to documented fully but see Anthony Carew, *Labour under the Marshall Plan* (Manchester: Manchester University Press, 1987) and Hugh Wilford, *The CIA, the British Left and the Cold War*

(London: Frank Cass, 2003) for examples of the US operations in the immediate post WWII era.

32. Subject of Frances Stonor Saunders, *Who Paid the Piper?* (London: Granta, 1999). For more details of the propaganda war waged by the US in the post 1945 era see Scott Lucas, *Freedom's War: The US Crusade Against the Soviet Union 1945–56* (Manchester: Manchester University Press, 1999).

33. See chapter 5 of Paul Rogers and Paul Landais-Stamp, *Rocking the Boat: New Zealand, the United States and the Nuclear-Free Zone Controversy in the 1980s* (Oxford: Berg, 1989).

34. This section of TUCETU is taken from David Osler's 'American and Tory intervention in the British unions since the 1970s' in *Lobster* 33.

35. A British organisation which hosts meetings of the Anglo-American and European political elite at Ditchley Park.

36. For the details of BAP membership see the essay by Tom Easton in *Lobster* 33. A shorter version of the same information is in John Pilger, *Hidden Agendas* (London: Vintage,1998) pp.96–7.

37. Another British site of meetings of the elite, funded by the Foreign Office. See Dexter M. Keezer, *A Unique Contribution to International Relations: the story of Wilton Park*, (Macgraw-Hill, Maidenhead, Berkshire, 1973).

38. Kenneth O. Morgan, *Callaghan: A Life* (Oxford: Oxford University Press, 1997) p.610. The 1974–77 operations are discussed in detail in Stephen Dorril and Robin Ramsay, *Smear! Wilson and the Secret State*

(London: Fourth Estate, 1991).

39. On his meetings with Thatcher and his intelligence career, see his memoir *Free Agent* (London: Harper-Collins, 1995).

40. See Paul Lashmar and James Oliver, *Britain's Secret Propaganda War 1948–1977* (Stroud, Glos.: Sutton Publishing, 1998). IRD was formally attached to the Foreign Office but grew in the 1950s and early 60s into a self-sustaining bureaucracy running its own policies.

41. See Peter Dale Scott, *Deep Politics II: essays on Oswald, Mexico, and Cuba* (Skokie, Illinois: Green Archive Publications, 1995).

42. The Venona decrypts were tape-recordings of radio traffic between the Soviet Embassy in the US and Moscow during the war. Moscow thought them unbreakable but was wrong. The US Army slowly broke a proportion of them and so learned of the extensive Soviet espionage network in the US. But this knowledge was kept secret until recently. See, for example John Earl Haynes and Harvey Klehr, *Venona: Decoding Soviet Espionage in America* (London: Yale University Press, 1999) and Allan Weinstein and Alexander Vassiliev, *The Haunted Wood* (New York: Random House, 1999).

43. On Angleton see the biography by Tom Mangold, *Cold Warrior* (London: Simon and Schuster, 1991).

It's the State, Dummy

In both the UK and the USA the military-intelligence complex, the national security state created during the Cold
War, works in secrecy and depends on secrecy for its survival in its current bloated form. This was nicely demonstrated in Britain by the story that between them MI5 and
MI6 were able to go £200 million over budget on their new
headquarter buildings in London, without the political system being aware of it.[1] Despite the fact that all the great
British traitors of the past century were professional intelligence officers, mere politicians are deemed not reliable
enough to be given access to 'the secret world'. In a sense,
the entire secret apparatus of the modern state – military,
policing, intelligence and security organisations – are simply state conspiracies and, all too frequently, are conspiracies directed against the taxpayers who fund them.[2]

The investigation of these state organisations and their
activities, which is essentially conspiracy research, but
which is more often called parapolitics, takes the official
account of reality and makes the world more complex.
Hundreds of books, half a dozen journals, who knows how
many websites and how many millions of pages of declassified material from the FBI and CIA on the Kennedy assassination alone have generated immense, almost
unmanageable complexity.[3] This is replicated, albeit to a

much lesser extent, in many of the big political scandals of the last twenty years. The documentation, for example, on the Iran-Contra affair, or the story of the British state's covert operations against the IRA, or the clandestine arming of Iraq, is now vast.

If conspiracy *research* complicates things, conspiracy *theories* simplify reality. The chaos of the world's economic system is reduced to a cabal of Jewish bankers. The US was in Vietnam because of the heroin in the Golden Triangle or at the behest of Howard Hughes who wanted to sell more helicopters. America is awash with drugs because of a communist conspiracy by the Soviets and/or the Chinese to undermine America. Britain is in economic decline because the KGB ran the unions which ruined Britain. The British Empire was lost because it was undermined by a conspiracy of communist traitors. And so forth. This simplification is undoubtedly part of the appeal of conspiracy theories. The world's ills are explained by the actions of this or that group or individual, and all the difficult, time-consuming complexity of real life, real politics – and real conspiracies – melts away.

All-embracing conspiracy theories are simply bad theories, held irrationally. Lyndon LaRouche and his followers have *no evidence* that the Queen runs the world's heroin traffic. There is *no evidence* that a secret Masonic cabal called the Illuminati has been running the world since the late 18th century. There is *no evidence* that the world's financial system is controlled by Jewish bankers. There is *no evidence* of a US government-alien conspiracy which began in the late 1940s. There is *no evidence* that the world's leaders are shape-shifting reptiles. Many such conspiracy theories barely deserve the description of 'theory' at all and are merely absurd claims.

The difficulty is that, in a sense, the people who are currently producing and recycling all the rubbish about global conspiracies, the David Ickes of this world, are right. But only in a sense. Some of the world's politics and economics *are* controlled by little groups of people. A friend of mine attended a conference of bankers in New York which was addressed by a big cheese from the US Federal Reserve who began his talk thus: 'Ladies and gentlemen, between us we control two thirds of the world's capital...' There *are* bankers ripping us off: the current world order has been designed by and for the benefit of bankers. But few of them are Jewish. The Bilderberg Group does exist and does meet. (The minutes of the 1999 meeting were leaked and posted on the Net. And were as anodyne as the minutes of a large meeting of people who don't know each other very well are likely to be.) The Trilateral Commission does exist and does discuss a new world order. After all, those attending such gatherings are the guardians and managers of transnational capital, and disorder is what they do not want. (It is bad for profits.) They may not want the New World Order of the paranoid fantasists on the American right but they certainly want order of some kind.

Mega-conspiracy theories are amusing – for a while. Unfortunately, their chief consequence is that they enable the powers-that-be to bracket people doing research into real conspiracies with those who believe that the Jews, the Illuminati, aliens, or shape-shifting reptiles[4] are running the world. David Icke, and the many Americans from whom he has adopted these ideas, pollute the subject matter, unwittingly playing into the hands of the very people they think they are opposing. The 'Jewish banking conspiracy' nonsense has, for half a century, served to make people nervous about researching the political power of finance capital in this society. The allegations floating around the so-called 'underground' press in the late 1960s and early 1970s that US policy in Vietnam was being run to benefit the heroin trade tended to discredit serious research in this area, notably Alfred McKoys' work on the role of US personnel in shipping opium for some of the mountain tribes who had been recruited to fight against the Vietcong.[5] The Illuminati nonsense makes academics and journalists dubious about the alleged influence of real groups such as Bilderberg.

Teaching Aliens to Line-dance

How do we tell which conspiracy theories or allegations of conspiracy are worth taking seriously? There are no special rules. The plausibility of a conspiracy theory is determined in the same way that any other proposition – or theory – is. It is all about weighing up reasons, rationality, weight of evidence. Just as in any other field, after a while, you get a 'feel' for what is and is not likely to be worth pursuing. In general, the larger the event allegedly explained by a conspiracy, the less likely it is going to be. We know what kinds of real conspiracies are routinely exposed: a government agency out of control; a bureaucracy covering-up something embarrassing; a witness threatened; people allegedly trying to influence a local council. These sorts of things are not improbable. Much less probable are the mega-conspiracies. The world being as strange as it is, it is difficult to say for certain that anything is impossible, but the odds on David Icke's vision of a world run by shape-shifting alien reptiles turning out to be true look very long. But other than something as bizarre as that, the boundaries of the plausible have been pushed out a long way, not least by some of the 'mind control' technology discussed below.

Take UFOs for example. It is preposterous to deny the existence of UFOs. There are too many reliable witnesses, too many former government officials from both sides of the former Iron Curtain who have acknowledged government interest in the subject, too many bits of film and videotape from all over the world. However, to move from a basic acknowledgement of their existence to the stories of abduction by alien sex fiends and the stories of an alien-US elite alliance stories which proliferated in the 1990s, is an enormous step. UFO's remain just that: *Unidentified* Flying Objects. That they exist cannot be rationally denied. But go beyond that basic statement and the evidence gets 'iffy' pretty quickly. There is no reliable evidence, of which I am aware, for the existence of aliens: no artifacts, no unchallenged photographs, no indisputable film, no videotape. There is only human memory, which is notoriously unreliable. If we are willing to treat human memory as 'evidence', we are likely to end up dealing with what we might call the 'Betty Trout Problem'.

Betty Trout is a State Director of the major American

UFO organisation MUFON. At MUFON's 1999 symposium she described how, in one of her abduction episodes, she noticed that the 'hybrids' – beings which are allegedly part alien and part human – among whom she was, appeared to be wearing cowboy boots and hats. Betty Trout taught line-dancing classes and she believed she had been abducted that evening to teach 'hybrids' to line-dance.[6]

The husband and wife team of Dr Helmut and Marion Lammer accept the legitimacy of human memory. In their book *MILABS* (Illuminet, 1999), they discuss accounts of alien abduction but emphasise those in which 'abductees' describe meeting normal (American) military personnel and, sometimes, 'aliens' working with normal military personnel, all of them conducting the same range of quasi-medical procedures on the 'abductees' as reported elsewhere. Having made this selection of the 'data' they offer as hypotheses the following:

> It seems to us that there are indications that more than one human agenda, possibly three, may be involved in the currently unexplained alien abduction phenomenon...one group may be interested in advanced mind-and-behaviour-control experiments...a second group seems to be interested in biological or genetic research...a third group seems to be a military task force, which has been operating since the 1980s...'[7]

The Lammers' book is an interesting piece of speculation but that is all it is. The Lammers chose to select 'abductees' who had 'seen' human soldiers or scientists. These 'abductees' are presumed to be reporting what they had 'seen' when they were, literally, abducted. But if these 'abductees' are reporting accurately, on what grounds do we determine that other 'abductees', who do not report seeing soldiers or scientists, are *not* reporting accurately? Would the Lammers accept, for example, that Betty Trout was literally abducted and did, literally, meet hybrids to teach them to line-dance? And if they would not, which criteria would they use to distinguish between Betty Trout's story and the stories they *do* believe?

The Lammers suspect that the experience of 'alien abduction' is being synthetically generated by state personnel for reasons unknown. Their book opens with a quotation from Dr. C. B. Scott Jones, quoted above. In 1994 Scott Jones had meetings with Dr. John Gibbons, the scientific advisor to President Clinton, at which various bits of evidence about UFOs were presented to Gibbons. On February 17 1994 Scott Jones wrote to Gibbons, *inter alia*:

> '…I urge you to take another look in the "UFO Matrix of Belief" that I provided you last year. My mention of mind-control technology at the February 4 meeting was quite deliberate. Please be careful about this. *There are reasons to believe that some government group has interwoven research about this technology with alleged UFO phenomena.* If that is correct, you can expect to run into early resistance when inquiring about UFOs, not because of the UFO subject, but because that has been used to cloak research and applications of mind-control activity.' (my emphasis added)[8]

Given Scott Jones' status and his years of access to high-level military, intelligence and political circles in the US, this comment of his is extremely interesting. But if he knows anything substantial about this 'mind control' experiment, he has chosen not to reveal it. On the other hand, if we do not believe that thousands of people (mostly Americans) have actually been abducted, how do we explain the fact that they have had *the experience* of being abducted other than by receiving an experience transmitted in some way?

Mind Control

Scott Jones referred to mind control experiments, one of the subjects which has generated a great deal of conspiracy theorising in the last decade. We know that the US military, the CIA, and their Soviet counterparts, were busy in the 1950s and 1960s looking for a means of controlling the human mind. Drugs, hypnosis and electromagnetic fields were all investigated by scientists funded by the US (and Soviet) taxpayer.[9] But there are now hundreds of people, in Europe and in the USA – I know someone dealing with over 100 such cases in the USA – who claim to have been the victims of mind control experiments. I have the written statements of half a dozen such 'victims' in this country. Some claim to have electronic devices implanted in their head, or their body; some claim they are being bombarded by energy weapons of some kind, mostly microwaves.

The distribution of victims suggests that, just as in the 1950s and the MK-Ultra/Delta programme, the American military farmed out bits of the experiments to other members of NATO. Canada features in some of the early reports, as does Sweden. I have seen X-rays which show implants in the brain of an individual in Sweden.[10] Brain scans are now available on home-pages on the Net, apparently showing the same sort of thing.

A Freedom of Information application by Jane Affleck produced a document from 1970, a report published by the Office of Technological Utilisation in NASA called Implantable Biotelemetry Systems – implants, in short. Thirty years ago they had them down to the size of a 5p piece. This 1970 report shows them and even provides wiring diagrams. Today, some of them are practically invisible, like a strand of hair. Or so it is said.

I have met three intelligent, educated people who tell me they hear voices in their heads – the voices of teams of psychologists and intelligence personnel monkeying around with their brains. (This is sometimes called synthetic telepathy.) I have corresponded with others. The stories of other, intelligent, apparently otherwise normal people who claim to be receiving the voices are available on the Net. I could just say they are paranoid schizophrenics, one of the classic symptoms of which is hearing voices in your head. But I have known some schizophrenics and these three people do not seem like schizos to me (and neither do the others whose accounts I have merely read). And here's the problem: even if they did sound nutty it still would be impossible to dismiss them because the technology exists to do what they claim is being done to them. As far back as 1962 an American scientist called Alan Frey demonstrated that, using a microwave beam, you could transmit sounds – words – into the head of an individual that were inaudible to other people: 'voices in the head'.[11]

There *are* people who have had implants put into their bodies and the evidence of this is now irrefutable. Microwave mind control devices *do* exist and, if the testimony of the alleged victims is to be believed, some of these devices do work as claimed. The US Patent Office contains shoals of systems for influencing or manipulating minds registered in the last 20 years and the systems the US state has decided are important to national security will *not* be in the Patent Office and we will never see them.[12] Before its collapse the Soviet Union was engaged in parallel research and there have been a series of reports in the last 15 years, from what is now Russia, suggesting that some of these devices have been deployed. Should we be surprised to learn that the CIA or some other branch of the US government (or its NATO allies) was doing random tests of this mind control technology? They did this with various nerve agents and experimental drugs in the fifties. They slipped them into peoples' drinks and just sprayed them round to see what happened. For the military scientists trying out their new weapons, their tests have the most perfect cover of all. No-one will believe the victims babbling about voices in the head or invisible rays. Though the victims of this technology have been complaining since the late 1980s, and the evidence of the technology is widely available on the Net, thus far the major media has declined to pay attention, preferring to dismiss the victims as crazies.[13]

I am not optimistic about this situation changing quickly. These technologies are now among the most sensitive of military/intelligence secrets and such secrets are difficult to expose. The CIA's early experiments in this field in the 1950s were kept secret until the late 1970s; the US government's various misuses of nuclear radiation in the United States in the early years of the Cold War were not addressed until Bill Clinton's first term; and the CIA's involvement in the drug trade, first described in the 1970s, was only reluctantly addressed in the late 1990s. In this country, apparently afraid of a torrent of compensation claims (or afraid to irritate the chemical lobby?), the government is unwilling to acknowledge that the use of organophosphates in sheep dip has seriously injured hundreds of farmers. (And both the US and the UK governments are unwilling to admit that the use of depleted uranium in the two Gulf wars has injured thousands of their soldiers and may have polluted areas of Iraq for centuries.) If dangerous chemicals in sheep dip is too awkward a subject for the British state to deal with, how much more reluctant will it be to acknowledge that some of its citizens have been the unwitting subjects of mind-control experiments by their employees or the employees of its allies, the Americans? Despite the enormous amount of scientific evidence now supporting their case, the victims of the mind control experiments of the last twenty years in the NATO countries are probably condemned to decades of marginalisation and ridicule.

David Icke

People who claim to 'hear voices' provide a good example of the difficulties that arise in this field once you start to try and assess such claims. I believe that some of these 'mind control victims' are what they say they are: unwitting subjects of military experiments. Since the technology to do this exists, they may be telling the truth. But I do not believe others. I do not believe those who claim that an operation called Operation Monarch turned them into the sex slaves of the rich and famous. There is no evidence of such an operation. The rich and famous hardly need mind-controlled zombies to fulfil their sexual desires (they can buy the services of others, if necessary) and the people making such claims seem flaky in the extreme. But others – and this is the distinction (I hope) between me and conspiracy theorists – take Operation Monarch at face value. One such is David Icke, now the most prominent conspiracy theorist in Britain and, perhaps, in the English-speaking world.

Icke's journey from Green Party activist in the 1980s to global conspiracy theorist has been one of the stranger journeys in recent years, its oddity only matched, perhaps, by that of Lyndon LaRouche Jr. who moved from being the leader of a US Trotskyist splinter group to a global conspiracy theorist who placed the British Royal family at the heart of his theories. I have tried and failed to read two of Icke's books – they are unreadable – but I managed to sit through most of an early video recording of him speaking in a theatre in Liverpool in (I think) the mid 1990s, before he discovered shape-shifting aliens. Even then Icke drew several hundred people, who paid to see him. As Icke strode around the stage, he lined up all our discontents, listed all the terrible things that are being done to the planet – the green element in his thinking – and discussed the catastrophe approaching. That took about fifteen minutes and, aimed as it was at an apolitical, mainstream audience, it was rather well done. He was a well known TV personality, after all. He's real, good looking and legitimised by his appearances on TV. He then asked the audience, not 'What is the cause or causes of this?', but 'Who is *behind* this?' Once you ask *that* question you're off into uncharted territory.

His answer then – his views have changed since – consisted of a mishmash of American conspiracy theories about semi-clandestine groups like the Trilateral Commission and the Council on Foreign Relation, a smattering of ufology's greatest hits, including the alleged existence of the super-secret US committee, Majestic 12, which deals with contact with aliens and the alleged alliance with the alien 'Greys', and old chestnuts like the influence of the Illuminati. Icke had continued the great American conspiracy tradition of adding new mega-conspiracy theories to the old ones. The conspiracy with the extra-terrestrials does not falsify or discredit the theory about the conspiracy by the Illuminati. Just add it on. The more the merrier! This makes life simple, of course, for audiences who are not used to handling evidence. The audience does not have to make the effort to decide if theory X has falsified and supplanted theory Y. All they have to do is add it to the list.

Before his adoption of the shape-shifting aliens I would have written of Icke that, like many of his American sources, his methodology was very basic. If it is in print, it must be true. But in fact it is worse – or better – than this. In an e-mail from the Icke org. about their on-line magazine, the following was given as the position of the org. on truth, falsehood and the nature of evidence.

> 'Each article [in the Icke e-zine] is presented to give everyone every possible source to TRUTH available. *Discerning TRUTH is the responsibility of each reader*. We welcome challenging viewpoints from all sources…even opposing viewpoints. In diversity of views we can still find the research and documentation valuable, whether we agree with the views of the author or not' (my emphasis added).

In other words, they are not interested in what is true and what is not or they have given up trying to work out which is which. This almost post-modern disdain for what used to be called 'objective reality' is common among contemporary conspiracy theorists. There may be rationales for distributing junk theories but the basic *reason* is simple enough. Most of the contemporary conspiracy theories would take months to check – if they were checkable at all – and almost all would be found to be false. If the hosts of conspiracy theory websites posted only what they knew or reasonably surmised to be true there would be little worth posting.

Notes

1. *The Independent* 18 February 2000.
2. The most recent British example of which I have personal knowledge concerns a man, wrongfully convicted of manslaughter who, now out of prison, is having his attempts to set up a small business disrupted by some branch of the state constantly blocking incoming telephone calls from potential customers. For the details of another such campaign see the account of the harassment of Armen Victorian in *Lobster* 29. Victorian's offence? He used the American Freedom of Information Act to request documents in areas the US military would rather were left alone.
3. An e-mail from Andy Winiarczyk at the Last Hurrah Bookshop in America, (tel. 570–321–1150) on Friday, 7 January 2000, gave details of 18 books (and one CD-ROM) on the JFK assassination I had not heard of, 6 published in the previous year.

   Kennedy buffs occasionally find themselves wondering if burying the researchers under mountains of paper isn't the objective of the declassification process.
4. As far as I am aware this is the current belief of David Icke.
5. This was later portrayed as comedy in the Mel Gibson, Robert Downey Jnr film, *Air America*. The film was very loosely based on a section of the book *The Invisible Air Force* by Christopher Robbins (London: Pan, 1981).
6. The Betty Trout story was reported in Kevin McClure's newsletter *Abduction Watch*, July 1999. AW

ceased publication in March 2000 but the extant issues are on line at *Magonia*'s site <www.magonia. demon.co.uk> If 'Betty Trout' sounds vaguely familiar you may be remembering the Kurt Vonnegut character Kilgore Trout.

7. Dr Helmut Lammer and Marion Lammer, *MILABS: Military Mind Control and Alien Abduction* (Lilburn, GA [USA]: Illuminet Press, 1999) p.29.

8. From Dr. C.B. Scott Jones, 'UFOs and new frontiers: connecting with the larger reality'. This was e-mailed to me, I don't know where it was first published and it isn't on the Net. On Scott Jones see Armen Victorian, *Mind Controllers* (London: Vision, 1999, pp.180–2).

9. The basic text on the American end of this remains John Marks, *The Search for the Manchurian Candidate* (Harmondsworth: Penguin Books, 1979). But see also Armen Victorian, see note 8 above.

10. The Swede is Robert Naeslund. The X-rays can be seen at <www.mindcontrolforums.com/v/robert-naeslund.htm>

11. See Armen Victorian, note 8 above, chapters 7 and 8.

12. For a survey of some US patents in this field see Armen Victorian, 'The military use of electromagnetic microwave and mind control weapons' in *Lobster* 34 which is reprinted in *Mind Controllers* (see note 8 above). See also 'Remote Behavioral Influence Technology Evidence', by John McMurtrey at <www.slavery.org.uk> This is the site of Christians against Mental Slavery.

13. David Hambling discussed the military operational use

of this, by the US, in the Science section of the *Guardian,* 3 February 2000.

Disinformation

The whole aim of practical politics is to keep the populace alarmed — and thus clamorous to be led to safety — by menacing it with an endless series of hobgoblins, all of them imaginary.
– H.L. Mencken

As well as being among the most important conspirators in the modern world, the secret arms of the state, the intelligence and security agencies (in the UK chiefly MI6 and MI5) have also been among the biggest generators of conspiracy *theories* since World War II. One of the skills they acquired during that war was black propaganda; and, with the onset of the Cold War, both sides began churning out disinformation about their opponents. Much of this was directed at contested areas in the developing world and is now difficult to trace. But sometimes the target audiences were in the West.

For example, in the wake of the Kennedy assassination both the Soviet and French intelligence services put out conspiracy theories about the killing. The Soviets spread their disinformation, blaming the CIA, through an Italian newspaper and thence into a French-language Canadian paper. From there it travelled into the JFK researcher community and eventually into the investigation of New Orleans District Attorney Jim Garrison (Kevin Costner in the movie *JFK*).[1] French intelligence personnel published a book, famous among JFK assassination buffs, called *Farewell America,* which also blamed the CIA for the shooting.[2]

For example, employees of the US, British and Israeli governments invented and spread the conspiracy theory that the KGB, using the Bulgarians, shot Pope John Paul II in 1981. Paul Henze, who wrote the first book proposing this theory, was a former CIA station chief (which was a bit of a clue!)[3] and the theme was taken up by other CIA assets, including the late journalist, Claire Sterling. In retaliation, the Soviets cooked up and spread the conspiracy theory that AIDS was a biological weapon developed by the US army designed to kill people of colour.[4]

Such disinformation operations can produce unanticipated problems. The 'KGB-shot-the-Pope' allegation was part of a wider disinformation operation run by US intelligence people in the early 1980s to portray the Soviet Union as the world's major sponsor of terrorism. Some of this material was fed out to selected friendly journalists, one of them being Claire Sterling who wrote it up as the 1981 book *The Terror Network.*[5] At this juncture the US Secretary of State Alexander Haig, who had made some bellicose speeches about the Soviets as sponsors of terror, asked the CIA to provide him with the evidence. Alas the CIA's 'National Intelligence Estimate' on the subject of Soviet sponsorship of terrorism failed to support Haig's charges. The Director of the CIA, William Casey, read the Sterling book and, unaware that the book was part of a CIA disinformation project, began complaining that the authors of the CIA's report on Soviet sponsorship of terrorism knew less about the subject than was in Sterling's book. I would like to have been there when this was explained to Casey.[6]

The British state had a organisation called the Information Research Department. It was set up originally in 1948, staffed with personnel from the war-time black propaganda organisations, with the stated aim of combating Soviet propaganda. But, as soon as the politicians' backs were turned, it reverted to what its employees knew best – disinformation. It survived until 1977, employing hundreds of people, barely noticed by the politicians, putting out unattributable (ie anonymous) briefings, some true, some grey (half true), and some black (false) through contacts in the print and broadcasting media made during the coldest parts of the Cold War. IRD turned up in all the post-war conflicts between the British colonial authorities and nationalist liberation movements in the British colonies, spreading the department 'line', its very own conspiracy theory: the commies are behind it all. And if there was no evidence that the Soviets were behind the troubles in – say – Cyprus or Northern Ireland, IRD would fabricate some.[7] In 1971 a senior member of the department was detached to Northern Ireland to work with the British Army there in the struggle against the IRA. He set up a psychological warfare unit called Information Policy which operated under cover of the press office in British Army HQ in Lisburn. Information Policy began putting out material – including forged documents – claiming that the KGB was behind the Provisional IRA and that the Labour Party was riddled with communists or fellow-travellers and supported the IRA.[8]

The disinformation war within the Cold War has yet to be looked at in any detail, but my guess would be that we will eventually discover that quite substantial chunks of what we thought was history has been faked.

Disinformation about UFOs

One recent area in which official disinformation was generated is UFOs. In British UFO magazines in 1996/7 we had a stream of tales of secret bases in Britain, aliens, dead bodies all over the place, and secret army units running round the UK, cleaning up the mess. Some of the accounts in these stories were not that far removed from a British version of the movie *Men in Black*, starring Will Smith and Tommy Lee Jones.[9] While claims of secret bases and secret units were a common feature of American UFO conspiracy theories in the decade before this, these stories were the first concerted attempt to get such themes established here. None of the stories was convincing and none of them 'took'. Secret bases are not wholly implausible in the United States because the deserts of the south-western states are so vast and so inaccessible that it is easy to imagine the US military hiding all manner of facilities down there. But in the UK this kite simply will not fly because the country is so small. None of these British stories appears to have been checked by the magazines concerned before publication – how you would convincingly check allegations of secret Army units is unclear to me – and, in all these stories, the sources of information were anonymous and nearly all claimed to be serving or former military personnel. One researcher in the field I know was even told that ancient and long discredited story, 'I'm a taxi driver and some big-wig left this briefcase in my cab'. In this version the briefcase was full of secret documents about the aliens and the government. Given that the researcher was ex-directory, he wondered how a London taxi-driver had got his number. The documents were not forthcoming, of course, and all the contact did was let him know that (a) a disinformation exercise was underway and (b) it was being run by incompetents.

That these themes of alien contact with the US government, or secret bases and technologies from the aliens were still being marketed in the mid 1990s is an indication of the success of US military and intelligence disinformation operations which ran from the mid 1970s onwards. The major operation we know of involved US Air Force personnel giving false information about UFOs, alien contact and subsequent conspiracies to four researchers in the field. Two of the four have described their experiences. A third had a nervous breakdown. The most important of them, the author Bill Moore, addressed the 1989 meeting of MUFON, the biggest grouping of people interested in UFOs in America, and told his audience that he had been working with US Army and intelligence officers to feed American UFO buffs – the audience he was addressing – a load of horse puckey about aliens, their landings, their meetings with government officials and secret deals. Much of the UFO agenda of the previous decade in America had been created by an inter-agency psychological warfare project with the US Air Force as the lead agency.

It began with Paul Bennewitz, an electronics manufacturer in New Mexico, who lived next to Kirtland Airforce Base, a vast complex in the New Mexico desert near Albuquerque. The Air Force was one of his customers. Bennewitz became fascinated by lights that he could see from his windows, moving around above some hills on the base. He began filming the lights, recorded their signals, and became convinced they were extraterrestrial in origin. Being a good US citizen (and an Air Force supplier), he took his discoveries to the base authorities. The US Air Force responded by pretending to believe him and then fed him disinformation about UFOs and the US government's alleged dealing with aliens. This disinformation was then circulated among UFO buffs in the US with the deadly *imprimatur,* 'From the US Air Force'. Along the way Bennewitz was introduced to a woman who claimed to have been abducted by aliens and a major league *folie à deux* was launched.

A great deal of 'modern ufology' (maybe most of it) over the last 20 years has been this rubbish run initially through Bennewitz. The author of the book about this episode[10] thinks that this disinformation began as a means of misdirecting Bennewitz away from secret US Air Force operations, but I wonder. The thing to do with an inquisitive businessman who makes his living selling electronic kit to the US government would be to say: 'You're a loyal American. All we can tell you is: *we can't tell you.*' Wave the national security flag and hint, if necessary, that his contracts might dry up. They didn't do this. They began misdirecting him, confirming his UFO theories.

Some of the same information that was given to

Bennewitz was given to Linda Moulton Howe, director of the film *Strange Harvest*, about another odd phenomenon of the South Western deserts of America, cattle mutilations.[11] In 1983 Howe was invited to the Kirkland Air Force Base where, in the Office of Special Investigations, she met one of its staff, Sergeant Richard Doty, the man who was feeding the disinformation to Paul Bennewitz. Doty told her that her film on cattle mutilations had 'upset some people in Washington' and, as a result, his superiors had asked him to brief her. She was shown a document called 'Briefing Paper for the President of the United States on the Subject of Identified Aerial Vehicles (IAVs)'. This contained a history of US Government retrieval 'of crashed disks and alien bodies, dead and alive'. The notorious Roswell incident was just one of several. But Howe was not allowed to make notes or copies of this document, just to read it.

Read-but-don't-copy was one of the disinformation techniques used by Colin Wallace in the British Army's psyops unit in Belfast in the 1970s.[12] Wallace would take journalists, especially foreign journalists with a limited understanding of British politics, into a back room and show them 'secret documents' which they could read but not copy. Some of the documents were genuine, some forgeries. We have copies of some of the forgeries.[13] Ms Howe was evidently unaware of this and began talking about her encounter with the US Air Force. We are all smarter than we were once but her willingness to give credence to this material was rather odd, for here apparently was the US Air Force, through a lowly non-commissioned officer, deciding to let her in on the story they had spent so much time and money previously trying to deny or rubbish in the preceding 40 years.

The second writer recruited was Bill Moore. By his own account, Moore was conned into joining the operation, being told it was a group of US intelligence professionals who wanted to leak more accurate information about UFOs to the public. Moore would be the conduit. (Or maybe he just couldn't resist what would obviously be a big story, whatever it turned out to be.) When he was recruited, Moore was a significant figure in the popular end of the paranomal/scientific mysteries writing world. He was the co-author of one of the big-selling books, the 1979 *The Philadelphia Experiment* and had just finished co-authoring what became another, *The Roswell Incident*.

In 1983, after some preliminary manoeuvres with the Air Force, checking out and feeding him small stuff, Moore received the MJ12 or Majestic papers, apparently documentary proof, from the government's own files, of the claims made by Sergeant Doty to Howe and Bennewitz. The MJ12 paper both described the various encounters with aliens and the bureuacratic structure which such encounters had produced. Here, apparently, was the 'cosmic Watergate' – a vast US government conspiracy to conceal contact, maybe even collaboration, with our alien neighbours. (Which many UFO buffs already believed was what had happened.) Moore eventually sat on the documents for more than two years while he and a colleague tried to check their claims, before letting the information out. To get Moore to stop sitting on the documents, he was told that another writer had the material and was threatening his 'scoop', and he duly released it at a UFO conference in 1987. (The UK's Timothy Good was the other person given the MJ12 material and used it in his 1987 book *Above Top Secret*.)

Having got their disinformation circulated among the world's UFO buffs, the Air Force proceeded to destroy it – a psy-ops technique Colin Wallace called 'the double bubble'. The target (in this case, American UFO researchers and/or the American media) is fed false but apparently convincing information which leads them down the wrong path (and possibly away from something that is sensitive). When the information has been established, the target is then told that the information they had accepted was false, was disinformation, thus leaving them confused. In this case the Air Force delivered a two-pronged puncture. The first was a 1988 nationwide TV show, *UFOs: Government Cover-up-Live*, which ran some of this alien material and included interviews with two of the disinformation network, in silhouette with their voices disguised, who made the stories seem ridiculous, telling their audience, *inter alia*, that the aliens liked strawberry ice-cream and Tibetan music.[14]

The second puncture was Bill Moore's confession to the assembled American UFO buffs in 1989. But the information didn't die. Some researchers simply didn't believe Moore. The aliens-contact-conspiracy story was *not* abandoned but, instead, it grew and grew, eventually going mainstream as the major underlying theme of *The X Files* TV programme. Sergeant Richard Doty of the US Air Force's Office of Special Investigations, who was the front man of this operation, eventually became a consultant on

The X Files for two years and even wrote the script of one episode. Air Force disinformation on global prime time!

It seems likely that the Bennewitz-Moore-Howe-MJ12 games were part of an existing disinformation operation. In 2001, a group of American former government employees, some military, announced at a press conference that they had all seen UFOs and called for congressional hearings on the subject. Acting as counsel for the group, the Disclosure Project, was Daniel Sheehan, best known for the 1986 'Affidavit of Daniel Sheehan', the most widely publicised aspect of the Christic Institute's failed attempt to get the alleged 'secret team' inside the US intelligence services into court.[15] At that press conference and later, in more detail, in a radio interview, Sheehan described a strange encounter with the US government over UFOs 14 years earlier.

Before becoming President in 1976, Jimmy Carter had been Governor of Georgia and, while Governor, had seen a UFO. He had even filed a report of the incident with one of the UFO monitoring groups.[16] Becoming President, Carter went to see the Director of the CIA, George Bush, and asked about UFOs. He was told by Bush that he didn't 'need to know' and would get nothing from the Agency. Bush suggested, however, that Carter approach the Congressional Research Service and ask them to prepare a briefing on the subject. As a result of this, says Sheehan, who was then General Counsel to the United States Jesuit National Headquarters in Washington, D.C., he was contacted by Marcia Smith, Director of the Science and Technology Division of the Congressional Research

Service. Sheehan was asked by Smith 'to participate in a highly classified major evaluation of the UFO phenomena, and extra-terrestrial intelligence'. She wanted Sheehan to get into the Vatican's files on the subject of UFOs. He tried and failed, even when the Vatican was told the query came from the US Congress. As a *quid pro quo*, perhaps, Sheehan then asked Smith if he could see the *classified* sections of the US Air Forces' study of UFOs, Project Blue Book. And this request was (apparently) duly granted.

Sheehan went into a room in the National Archives and was told he could look but not take notes. (Does this injunction sound familiar?)

'There were a bunch of documents there. There was actually a film machine. It was like a little reel-to-reel-kind of a film machine there. I don't know if it was 35mm, or whatever those things were. So there was actually some little films there. I looked at some of the films and they were like the classic films that you have seen, sort of far distant shots of strange moving vehicles. So I decided I wasn't making much headway on this, so I began to look into these little boxes, that had these canisters there...I had gone through several, or at least a few of these boxes, when I hit upon this one canister that had film and pictures. I started going through, turning the little crank and there it was...There were these photographs of unmistakable – of a UFO sitting on the ground. It had crashed, apparently. It had hit into this field and had dug up, kind of plowed this kind of trough through this field. It was wedged into the side of this bank. There was snow all around the picture. The vehicle was wedged into the side of this mud-like embankment kind of up at an angle. There were Air Force personnel. As I cranked the little handle, and looked at additional photos, these Air Force people were taking pictures. In the photograph they were taking photographs of this vehicle. One of the photos actually had the Air Force personnel with this big long tape measure measuring this thing. You could see that they had these parkas on, with little fur around their hoods. You could see that they had the little name tags on their jacket. They were clearly U.S. Air Force personnel. I was kind of in this strange state saying, "Here it is!"

So I turned the crank for more pictures, and I could see on the side of this craft these like little insignias – little symbols. So I turned ahead a couple of pictures to see if there was a closer picture. Sure enough there was. One of the photos had kind of a close-up picture of these symbols. So what I did is, I was getting nervous. I looked around, and the guys [security personnel] weren't watching or anything. They were outside of the room, so I took the yellow legal pad, and I flipped it open to the little grey cardboard backing and I flipped it under the screen. I shrank the size of the picture to the exact same size as the back of the yellow pad, and traced the actual symbols out in detail, verbatim of what was there...Once I had actually seen these pictures, and actually chosen to copy down and trace these symbols from this craft, I just decided that I should get out of there. So I got up, closed the little pad, and I put the film back in the canister. I put all the boxes back where they were, and put the yellow pad under my arm, and just walked out. As I came through the door, I went over to get my briefcase up, and the man at the little desk that was sitting there pointed to the yellow pad under my arm, and he said, "What's that that you've got there?" I said, "That's the yellow pad that I had with me." He said, "Let me see that." He reached out and I handed it to him. He flipped through the yellow pages, and never looked at the back, never looked at the inside cardboard backing, and handed it back to me. So, I just put it under my arm, got my briefcase and walked out of there.'[17]

And didn't say anything in public for 14 years...

As presented by Sheehan, this episode is absurd. A request from the Congressional Research Service would not give Sheehan access to classified material. Sheehan was given access to disinformation; the 'look but don't take notes' instruction is standard psy-ops. This suggests that the disinformation operation which apparently began with Paul Bennewitz in 1980, and moved on via Linda Moulton Howe to Bill Moore and the Majestic documents, has its origins further back than we had previously known. It may be that the failure of Sheehan to publicise what he had seen led the people running the project to try again with Bennewitz, Moore and Howe.

The purpose of the various disinformation operations in the UFO field is unclear. They may simply be re-running the operations of the 1950s in which the CIA and other government agencies encouraged the belief in UFO sightings to provide 'cover' for their secret aircraft. (Seen a bright shining object high in the sky, Mildred? It is a UFO, not a U-2 spy-plane on its way to photograph the Soviet Union at 65,000 feet.)[18]

This has been suggested as the explanation for the strange events at Area 51, Groom Lake, the US Air Force's testing base in the desert. Better to have the curious visitor think he or she has seen a collection of UFOs flying at night over the mountains which surround the base than believe the US is testing a variety of experimental planes about which Congress has not been informed. The Area 51 story over the past 15 years or so bears all the hallmarks of a disinformation exercise: leaks, dribbles of information, many stories from putative employees at the base and one apparently authoritative witness, Jim Lazar, who, upon closer scrutiny, starts to look less solid than he did at first.[19]

Dr. C. B. Scott Jones, one of the people most closely involved in the curious area where UFO researchers meet politicians and the military-intelligence complex, offered this as an explanation of the disinformation operations.

'Earlier I asked the question why there was no press response to Reagan's extraordinary statements concerning a space threat to the world. The short answer is that the press has effectively been taken out of the loop by the success of a counter-intelligence program targeted against the American public and the press. The government wants no restrictions on how it attempts to handle what we are calling UFO phenomena. To get this freedom of action, a clamp of secrecy and stealth intimidation of the press has been employed. The program has been so successful against the press, that it doesn't even recognise the wound. The process apparently was to stage a number of 'UFO events', get the press charging to the bait and then with fanfare show that it was either a hoax or misinterpretation of natural phenomena. [The 'double bubble' technique – RR.] When print editors hear: 'UFO, UFO', we get the same response from them that the village finally gave the young sheep herder who cried 'Wolf' too many times.'[20]

Notes

1. This was first exposed by Stephen Dorril, in an essay in *Lobster* 2. This is now available on the Web at <http://mcadams.posc.mu.edu/lobster.htm>

2. I asked a retired SIS officer who his circle thought had done the deed when they first heard of it in 1963. 'The CIA,' he said. This was also apparently the belief of the Kennedy family.

3. *The Plot to Kill the Pope* (Beckenham, Kent: Croom Helm, 1984).

4. On the disinformation about the shooting of the Pope see Edward S. Herman and Frank Brodhead, *The Rise and Fall of the Bulgarian Connection* (New York: Sheridan Square Publications, 1986).

   According to a 2005 State Department bulletin on how to spot disinformation: 'In March 1992, then Russian foreign intelligence chief Yevgeni Primakov admitted that the disinformation service of the Soviet KGB intelligence service had concocted the false story that the AIDS virus had been created in a US military laboratory as a biological weapon.' <http://usinfo.state.gov/media/Archive/2005/Jul/27-595713.html>

   The AIDS-as-bio-weapon story was convincingly traced back to Soviet intelligence before this admission. See, for example, Christopher Andrew and Oleg Gordievsky *KGB: the Inside Story* (London: Hodder and Stoughton, 1990), pp.528–9 and *Counterpoint: a monthly report on Soviet Active Measures*, Vol. 3 no. 6, November 1987.

5. Sterling died in 1995. See the obituaries in the *Independent* 26 June 1995 and the *Guardian* on 29 June. Sterling was certainly an intelligence asset, and possibly even a CIA officer. The best response to her Terror Network nonsense was Edward Herman's *The Real Terror Network* (Boston: South End Press, 1982) which showed, without a great deal of difficulty, that the major sponsor of terrorism in the post-war years has been the United States.

6. This is discussed in James Der Derian, 'Anti-diplomacy, Intelligence Theory and Surveillance Practice' in Wesley K. Wark (editor) *Espionage: Past, Present, Future*, (London: Frank Cass, 1994).

7. For an example from the Cyprus war see Charles Foley, *Legacy of Strife: Cyprus from rebellion to civil war* (Harmondsworth: Penguin, 1964) p.104.

8. On this see Paul Foot, *Who framed Colin Wallace?* (London: Macmillan, 1990). Some of the forgeries are reproduced in this volume.

9. See for example, '580 Security' in *Global UFO Investigation* June/July 1997; 'UFO crash in North Wales', *UFO*, September/October 1996; the untitled essay in *Unopened Files* No 1, pp. 5–19; 'Programmable Life Forms' in *Truth Seekers Review* no. 9. Thanks to Kevin McClure for bringing these to my attention.

10. On Bennewitz see Greg Bishop, *Project Beta* (New York: Paraview, 2005). It is possible that the climax of this operation was the 'discovery' of the notorious film apparently showing an alien autopsy but there is no evidence linking that piece of film to the documents. (And if the deception operation was any good, no such evidence will ever be found.)

11. On Ms. Howe's story see C. D. B. Bryan, *Close Encounters of the Fourth Kind,* (Harmondsworth: Penguin, 1996) pp.102–125.

12. Wallace described this to the author. IRD used this technique in Cyprus. See the reference in note 7 above.

13. Some of these are reproduced in Paul Foot's *Who Framed Colin Wallace?*

14. Bishop (see note 10) pp.211–2.

15. A very short account of the Christic Institute by Daniel Brandt is at <www.namebase.org/sources/LX.html> See also <www.skepticfiles.org/socialis/contrarv.htm> for a longer account. Christic's lawsuit against this 'secret team' was thrown out by the first judge who considered it.

16. On the Carter story see 'Untold history – The Jimmy Carter UFO agenda' at <http://groups.yahoo.com/group/Skyopen/message/6618?viscount=100>

17. Sheehan's tale is at <www.ufominbd.com/ufo/updates/2001/jul/m16-015.shtml>

18. See the CIA's own report on this, Gerald K. Haines, 'CIA's Role in the Study of UFOs, 1947–90' at

<www.cia.gov/csi/studies/97unclass/ufo.html>
19. Go to <www.serve.com/mahood/lazar/lazarmn.
    htm> for a long, detailed, sceptical analysis of Lazar.
20. From Dr. C. B. Scott Jones, 'UFOs and new frontiers:
    connecting with the larger reality'. This was e-mailed
    to me, I don't know where it was first published and it
    is not on the Net.

Conspiracy *Theories* and Conspiracies

There is a right and a left political dimension to this. In very broad terms, the right, historically, has been interested in conspiracies it perceives to be undermining some kind of natural or desired order, plotting against the will of the people, the constitution, the national interest etc. These are what we might loosely call conspiracies *against* the state. The communist conspiracy theory, the Jewish banker theory and the current crop of New World Order, One World, elite dominance theories are examples of this. The liberal-left, on the other hand, has been chiefly interested in conspiracies committed *by* the state. From where I am, on the left side of the fence, quite why these two areas are so distinct is unclear to me: an interest in the elite management groups (right) should fit comfortably with an interest in the big state scandals – say Iran-Contra (left). In practice, however, the right's desire to preserve – or conserve – the existing order, no matter how critical they may also be of it, has generally precluded them from acknowledging the crimes and conspiracies of that order. On the other side, the left is unwilling to engage with a subject matter which has been 'contaminated' by interest from the right. Look at the almost complete lack of interest shown by the American left in the massacre of the Branch Davidians by federal forces at Waco, Texas.[1]

The liberal-left strand of interest in conspiracies by the state begins with the Kennedy assassination in 1963, and the killings of Robert Kennedy and Martin Luther King in 1968, and, from there, runs seamlessly through the Vietnam War, into Watergate and then into all the related revelations of CIA and FBI operations which followed Watergate. If you started now and devoted yourself full-time to getting up to speed on the literature on the JFK killing alone it would take a year, maybe more.[2] Let us go back, briefly, to 1963 and see if we can get a sense of why these assassinations of almost 40 years ago are not only relevant but seminal.

In 1963 there was virtually no investigative journalism. Indeed, large chunks of the US mass media had been co-opted by the CIA into the propaganda war with the Soviet Union.[3] There was little American left and much of what there was thoroughly penetrated by the FBI and local police forces.[4] The conspiracy theory writer, Robert Anton Wilson, described his experiences of this:

In the 1960s in Chicago, I was involved in the anti-war movement. Congressional investigators later revealed that there were over 5,000 government agents assigned to in-filtrate peace groups in Chicago alone, some working for the Federal Bureau of Investigation (FBI), some for the Central Intelligence Agency (CIA) and some for Army Intelligence. From 1968 on, the FBI was following a pro-gram code-named COINTELPRO. The purpose of COIN-TELPRO was to make sure the anti-war movement knew it was infiltrated, in order to spread suspicion, distrust and paranoia among individuals and groups who might otherwise have co-operated harmoniously. Working in the peace movement in those days was, accordingly, like living in an Eric Ambler novel. In any given week I would be warned perhaps three times that somebody I trusted was really a government agent, and, of course, somebody who was accused one day might very well be around to accuse somebody else the next day. Over 20 years later, I still don't know who was a government agent and who was not. [5]

There was, in fact, little critical community of any kind in the USA in 1963. Those who went through the motions of sitting on the Warren Commission, investigating the Kennedy assassination, assumed that they would produce a report which no one would read and the whole thing would then be put to bed. Since the whole thing was, if not a charade, then a less-than-serious attempt to get at the truth, the evidence haphazardly accumulated by the Commission's team of lawyers was thrown together higgledy-piggledy in the Warren Commission's famous 26 volumes of evidence, with no sense, no organisation and no index worth speaking of. It just never occurred to those in charge that anyone would bother to look. One of the Commission members, former CIA chief Allen Dulles, famously said of the Report that it would only be read by a few professors. He was wrong. A number of ordinary US citizens who felt the official version of the assassination was dodgy, to say the least, bought one of the 1,000 copies of the evidence which the government had printed and then began poring over it. One woman indexed the 26 volumes. Almost immediately the shoddy nature of the investigation was revealed.

The Warren Commission and its team of lawyers were *not* tasked to investigate the shooting of JFK but to provide the evidence that Oswald, the 'lone nut', had done it. We now know that one of the chief preoccupations of those in charge in the White House at the time was preventing the assassination being used by anti-communist pressure groups within the US – the anti-Castro Cubans, in particular – to trigger another invasion of Cuba by US forces. Within 24 hours of the shooting, the Attorney General, Nicholas Katzenbach, had decided that the whole thing had better be shut down. In the collective Washington memory, the Cuban Missile Crisis of 1962 still loomed large. In that climate, who really shot Kennedy was never an issue. As far as we can judge from the memoirs of those around at the time, nobody seems to have cared greatly. The identity of Kennedy's killer was of little consequence when measured against the danger of another nuclear showdown with the Soviet Union. [6]

The federal government's major investigative body, the FBI, was happy that there was to be no serious investigation because they were in danger of being exposed as grossly incompetent. If it was shown that Oswald, *qua* communist, had done the deed for political reasons, then they had failed to prevent a communist shooting the President. And there was the danger that Oswald would be revealed as an FBI informant, for which there is some evidence. So the 'lone nut' verdict suited the politicians, who did not want trouble with the Soviet Union. It suited the FBI – how could they be blamed for the actions of a madman? It also suited the other American agencies, including the CIA, with whom Oswald had been involved in his curious career. [7]

In the big assassinations of the 1960s, the Kennedys and King, the conspiracy hinged on presenting the forces of law and order with a ready-made solution. Oswald was framed, but framed so crudely it is pretty obvious he was meant to be a dead assassin. What they had against him would never have stood up in court; and had he appeared in court he would have talked of his various intelligence roles.

In the killing of Martin Luther King the police were again involved. The patsy, James Earl Ray, was run around America, told to buy a rifle, and finally installed in a boarding house near the site of the shooting. The local police detailed to guard King were pulled off and King was shot. The rest was easy because the local police found a rifle and other bits and pieces linked to James Earl Ray, conveniently left near the scene of the crime. *Voila!* Case closed. Everybody in Memphis law enforcement was happy – everybody, that is, except a black cop guarding King, who had been called away just before the shooting. James Earl Ray, threatened with the death penalty if he was tried and convicted, accepted a plea bargain and confessed to something he hadn't done. So, there was no trial and the evidence against Ray was not tested. Again, as with the JFK murder, there was no serious investigation by the authorities. [8]

With the Robert Kennedy murder it was more sophisticated. In that one the patsy assassin did actually shoot at Kennedy in front of dozens of witnesses. Yet the American political and judicial system's refusal to take on board the

RFK assassination is even more perverse than in the case of his brother. The autopsy evidence is absolutely clear that Robert Kennedy was shot at point-blank range behind his ear: his skin had power burns indicating a firing distance of no more than a couple of inches. But Sirhan, all eyewitnesses agree, was in front of him and never got close enough to inflict that wound. The obvious other candidate is a man called Thane Cesar who was working as a temporary security guard and was standing right behind Kennedy when he was shot. Robert Kennedy whirled round and tried to grab Cesar when he was shot. One of the pictures of Kennedy dying on the floor in the hotel kitchen, shows Cesar's bow-tie on the floor next to him. Kennedy had ripped it off. Cesar denies he did it and passed a lie-detector test on the question – if that means anything.[9]

The official verdicts remain that Oswald, Ray and Sirhan did the deeds, although the 1977 House Select Committee on Assassinations hedged their bets a little and concluded that John F. Kennedy was probably killed by a conspiracy. Having spent at least a decade in bed with the CIA, the major American media needed little persuading to accept the US government's 'lone assassin' verdict in JFK's case. The other two assassinations seemed clear-cut. Ray confessed and Sirhan was seen firing at RFK.

All three assassinations hinged on local police forces either co-operating in the murders or not doing their jobs properly. All three relied on the major media and the political system not asking questions. It is one of the striking political facts of post-war American history that the Democratic Party lost its two most charismatic figures and

never generated much of a head of steam for a decent inquiry. Had it not been for the handful of sceptics back in
the 1960s poring over the Warren Commission evidence,
the whole thing would have slipped into history just as
Allen Dulles predicted.

The group of JFK assassination researchers in the 1960s
chipped away at the Warren Commission, dismantling the
report section by section. More importantly, in doing so,
they embarked on a long process of self-education about
the nature of US politics and post-war history. This, in
turn, brought to the public's attention the role of agencies
like the CIA which had hitherto been largely secret. By the
time what became known as Watergate began to break in
1973, the majority of the American electorate had ceased
to believe the Warren Commission and many were prepared to believe that the American government was capable of almost anything. (Tens of thousands of bodies of dead
American soldiers returning from Vietnam helped.)

The Kennedy assassination was the lens through which I,
along with many other people, first began to study
American politics. For the Kennedy assassination said here
is a society and a political system in which the President is
shot in broad daylight and the body politic – his professional
colleagues – did not feel able to look for the truth. No
doubt part of that reluctance was engendered by the com-
petition with the Soviet Union and the significance of this
factor, in the minds of those in Washington who created the
'lone assassin' myth, was underestimated at the time by the
first wave of JFK researchers. However the central point
remains: 22 November 1963 was the moment when the

collective post-war innocence of the American Dream ended and conspiracy research began.[10] Which is why the shots of that day in Dallas are still ringing in the ears of the American public.

Conspiracies are real and by no means necessarily the product of a paranoid imagination. If this little book has a single message, this is it. But, as the Kennedy assassination showed, there is not just one big over-arching conspiracy. There are many smaller conspiracies, some of them competing, interlocking, overlapping. Lee Harvey Oswald had documented connections to the FBI and the CIA and his activities have led to serious research into whole areas of covert operations by both agencies about which the US public and political system was almost entirely ignorant in 1963. One example is the FBI's COINTELPRO operations against the American left. Oswald's one-man branch of the Fair Play for Cuba Committee in New Orleans was probably – but not yet provably – a part of the COINTELPRO operations against the national pro-Castro Fair Play for Cuba Committee. Jack Ruby was an FBI informant in the early 1950s and was the payoff man between organised crime and the Dallas Police. Had there been a half-serious investigation of Kennedy's shooting in 1963/4, Oswald and Ruby alone would have led to the CIA's then still officially secret war against Cuba run out of Miami, the anti-Castro alliance formed between the CIA and the Mafia, and the FBI's COINTELPRO operations. When Ruby shot Oswald all these organisations had reasons to cover up the truth about their connections to both men. There *was* a conspiracy to murder Kennedy but there were many conspiracies after his death to suppress the truth and mislead the investigations which had nothing to do with the initial assassination conspiracy. It took many years for the JFK assassination research buffs to see past the idea that, by researching the cover-up, they would follow the trail back to the conspirators. There were too many cover-ups and too many trails. The *cui bono?* (who benefits?) question told us nothing in either the Oswald or Kennedy murder cases: a great many people and political forces in America benefited from both deaths.

These observations about the nature and meaning of bureaucratic cover-ups – essentially that every unaccountable bureaucracy, such as the FBI or CIA, has much to hide and the fact of a cover-up does not necessarily imply other guilt – have not been taken on board by some of those who suspect that 9/11 was a conspiracy by Americans, not al-Qaeda. Look, they say, the official 9/11 inquiry is inadequate and full of holes and signs of cover-up. But the Kennedy assassination material shows that such official inquiries are always inadequate, that the object of such an inquiry is to head-off criticism and real inquiry, and to cover the backsides of the state bureaucracies and politicians involved. Official inquiries are *political* processes and politics isn't interested in the truth.

A Conspiracy Culture?

At the beginning of this chapter I suggested, loosely, that the liberal-left was interested in conspiracies *by* the state and that the conservative-right was interested in conspiracies *against* the state. The distinction is still meaningful but the categories are less neat and tidy than they seemed in 1996 when I began writing the talk which became the outline of the first edition of this book. It seems to me that there are increasing numbers of people writing in the fields of conspiracy theory and conspiracy research whose political affiliations are difficult to determine, who are neither right nor left but who are (apparently) simply conspiracy theorists. Some years ago, *Steamshovel*, which began as a magazine somewhere on the anarchist left, announced its new, improved website with the slogan 'all conspiracy, no theory'. And where would you place Jonathan Vanakin, author of *Conspiracies, Cover-ups and Crimes*, perhaps the best single volume guide to this field? Or Tony Gosling, this country's leading researcher into the Bilderberg group, whose website on the group includes sections on his Christian beliefs? Or <www.rense.com>, perhaps the leading American conspiracy site, named in a 2005 State Department bulletin giving advice on how to spot disinformation? There is nothing obviously left-wing about rense.com and much of its agenda – New World Order, alternative medicine – has historically been associated with the radical right but its willingness to believe that the US state (and states in general) are capable of any calumny is a view that, until fairly recently, was to be found only on the left. Some on the political right have joined the left in identifying the state as the conspirator-in-chief. In the first edition of this book, written in 2000, I wrote that I thought an 'ideologically neutral conspiracy theory mindset, a conspiracy theory culture' was implausible. Five years on I'm not so sure.

Another change in the last decade – since the Internet – has been the apparent decline in the visibility of the 'Jewish' conspiracy theory. While the theme of the 'Jewish' conspiracy is still running strongly in the Middle East (thanks to American support for Israel), in the Anglo-American world, thanks in part to the seriously strange stuff of the last decade (aliens, abductions and Icke), the 'Jewish' conspiracy theory has become just one among many in the great conspiracy pick-and-mix menu. In the (almost) free market in ideas and beliefs which the English-language Net offers those who have access to it, the Jewish conspiracy theorists seem to be losing ground. For many people, especially younger people, 'conspiracy theory' does not resonate with the sound of gas chamber doors closing.

Hits on the Internet's primary search engine Google isn't proof of anything but the following relative numbers are nonetheless suggestive. Using the formula 'X + conspiracy' I got these results from Google searches in September 2005:

- New World Order 14,700,000
- Mind control 7,010,000
- 9/11 5,710,000
- CIA 2,770,000
- Jews 2,420,000
- JFK 1,030,000

Would you have predicted that in the conspiracy 'hit parade' the Jews would be less important than the CIA? I didn't.

The other interesting thing about that Google 'hit parade' is the big figures for the mind control and 9/11 categories. I have looked at an infinitesimal proportion of those sites but even the briefest glimpse at a few will show that the underlying belief of both groups is that the government – more accurately the state – in western democracies is the problem. It is the state which is experimenting with mind control technology. It is the state, the 9/11 theorists argue, which organised the plane bombings of America or let them happen.

The Net makes our masters nervous. That fact that the US State Department actually put out a statement on how to spot disinformation, naming rense.com (and the late Joe Vialls)[11] is evidence of that. The problem for the state is that the Net speeds up the dissemination of information enormously and this makes it difficult for the state to control public perceptions in the ways it once did. The US-UK disinformation campaigns about Iraq's weapons of mass destruction, in the run-up to the invasion of Iraq, were spotted and dismantled by people using the Net. There were conspiracy theorists on the Net announcing that it was obvious that 9/11 was a stunt done by the Americans themselves – an 'American Reichstag Fire' was the expression used then – within *24 hours* of the event. One of the first big developments of the 9/11 conspiracy theories came from some comments by a demolition expert that the way the Twin Towers fell looked like a controlled demolition. Published in the *Albuquerque Journal* in New Mexico on the day of the attacks, these were spotted and circulated world-wide the next day.[12]

9/11 is the big enchilada of current political conspiracy theories. A few days after the event, Anthony Frewin, like me a student of the Kennedy assassination literature, suggested that 9/11 was going to be the JFK assassination for the Internet generation. It would be the seminal event which kicks off a generation of researchers. It certainly seems that way. But while the 9/11–JFK comparison *is* plausible, there are two big differences. Kennedy was just a politician and killing politicians in the United States is not *that* unusual. What the 9/11 conspiracy theorists are suggesting is either that the US authorities – at some, as yet unspecified, level – knew the attack was coming and let it happen or that it was organised by them. If either of those conspiracy theories about 9/11 is established, this is infinitely bigger than the killing of Kennedy.

The second difference between now and 1963 is the existence of the Net itself. By comparison with the JFK event, there is infinitely more information and speculation available. An army of volunteers scans the media and attempts to summarise and synthesise the torrent of information. Every little wrinkle, anomaly and leak is immediately made available. With JFK the critics had to wait for the publication of the official version, Warren Commission in 1964, then go through that – indeed index it first – and only then find somewhere to publish articles or books. The Kennedy assassination sceptics didn't get going until 1966 and the publication of the books by Harold Weisberg (*Whitewash*), Mark Lane (*Rush to Judgement*) and Edward Epstein (*Inquest*), more than two years after the assassination; and didn't *really* get going until the mid 1970s and the explosion of revelations about the CIA and FBI after Watergate. In late June 2002 '9/11 conspiracy' produced 42,300 hits on Google. That was a mere nine months after the attack. On the analogy with the JFK assassination, the 9/11 sceptics had done in a week what it took the JFK researchers three years to do. After nearly 40 *years* the literature on the JFK assassination (hundreds of books, millions of pages of declassified government documents, hundreds of websites) is almost too big to deal with. After 6 *months* the Net material on 9/11 was too big to deal with and, in September 2005, the same formula on Google, '9/11 conspiracy', produced over 5 *million* hits. [13] On the other hand, where the material criticising the official version of the Kennedy assassination – most of it anyway – had to be run past editors of one kind or another before hard copy publication, the Internet is mostly editor-free and a lot of what is posted is just rubbish. Of those 5 millions hits, how many are going to be worth examining?

In one other aspect 9/11 and JFK are similar. Even if the sceptics produce unanswerable evidence of conspiracy and official cover-up, as they did with JFK, it still remains to persuade the political system and the major media that this is something which should be pursued. More than forty years after JFK's death there is still no significant political lobby supporting a decent inquiry and, despite all the enormous effort by the 9/11 sceptics, only one significant American politician, a black congresswoman, has shown any public interest. There is thus the possibility that the 9/11 sceptics, like the JFK researchers, will spend 40 years being ignored by the powers-that-be.

Concluding Comments

Conspiracy theories appeal to different groups for different reasons. They provide cheap – and safe – television programmes. Serious current affairs, let alone investigative journalism, is expensive and seen by TV executives as legally dangerous. Conspiracy theories can always be presented as 'X thinks Y', rather than 'X did Y'. They are the soft option and not just for those making TV programmes. Conspiracy theories do not require the audience to do any more than ogle. Some of them – who killed Di and Marilyn and JFK? – are sexy: it's a kind of celebrity history. It's whodunits and people with really weird ideas – few of which suggest that you should actually do anything. It has some of the appeal of the freak show. Some of it is almost apolitical politics and it is that apolitical aspect which irritates so many liberal-left commentators.

The commercial success of Michael Moore's film *Fahrenheit 9–11* – \$150 million plus at the box office – provoked another wave of conspiracy-bashing. [14] Moore may look like some kind of left-winger on this side of the Atlantic, but, to the American left, he looks like something quite different. He looks like what the Americans call a conspiracist and the American left hates conspiracists. Here's a well known American left writer, Norman Solomon, on the dangers.

'[conspiracism] encourages people to fixate on the spectre of a diabolical few plotters rather than on the profoundly harmful realities of ongoing structural, institutional, systemic factors.' [15]

And here's Chip Berlet of Political Research Associates, writing in the context of the explosion of conspiracy theories about 9/11:

'People with unfair power and privilege generally try to hold onto that unfair power and privilege. Sometimes they make plans that are not publicly announced. Sometimes they engage in illegal plots. Real conspiracies have been exposed throughout history. History itself, however, is not controlled by a vast timeless conspiracy. The powerful people and groups in society are hardly a "secret team" or a tiny club of "secret elites"...conspiracism impedes attempts to build a social movement for real social justice, economic fairness, equality, peace, and democracy.' [16]

In other words, conspiracy theories are a distraction and a form of false consciousness. Clearly this is, in a sense, true. Somebody who is pursuing alien abductions probably isn't reading Marx – or Chip Berlet. But in their desire to turn us back towards decent, respectable leftism – 'a social movement for real social justice, economic fairness, equality, peace, and democracy' – Berlet and Solomon fudge some important distinctions. 'A vast timeless conspiracy', 'all major world events as primarily the product of a secret conspiracy', 'a secret team', 'a tiny club of "secret elites"' and 'a diabolical few plotters' are not the same thing. The notion of a secret team was first used by an American army officer, the late L. Fletcher Prouty in a specific context: he saw an unofficial group, a network, within the CIA. Other people, the Christic Institute for example, during the Reagan administration, have claimed to see something similar. (Of the two, Prouty's case is much more convincing.) In the London Metropolitan Police a network of corrupt police officers in the 1970s was known as 'the firm within a firm'. A 'secret team' is just a step away from the older term, secret society. In Italy in the 1980s, the Masonic lodge P2 was precisely 'a secret team' or a secret society. As for 'a tiny club of secret elites', there are elite groups, some of which are secret – or would like to be secret (Bilderberg, Bohemian, Le Cercle for example) but, to my knowledge, no-one has ever described them as being a 'club', big or small. As for 'a vast timeless conspiracy' and 'all major world events as primarily the product of a secret conspiracy', these are beliefs held by relatively few in the English-speaking world and are of no political consequence.

Berlet and Solomon *et al* are making intellectual and political mistakes. They are simply wrong to regard political conspiracies – even secret societies – as insignificant. Rather than berating conspiracy theorists for their false consciousness, they would surely be better applauding their perception that the world isn't as it is presented by the corporate media, and trying to encourage them towards the more rational areas of conspiratorial thinking and an understanding of how conspiracies fit into the wider structure of American society. There is no intrinsic conflict between being interested in the study of the structural inequalities of western democracies and conspiracies. They are – indeed could and should be – complementary, parts of the critical armoury.

Political conspiracy is so routine, the concept of conspiracy would be of little interest were it not for the refusal of our chattering classes to acknowledge its legitimacy. On the other hand, that people interested in what our elites are doing can be dismissed as anoraks, conspiracy theorists and – the British journalists' favourite – 'people with an agenda', is very useful to our rulers. [17]

The importance of conspiracies, not conspiracy *theories*, is political. The conspiracies we should be looking at most closely are those run by the state – in this benighted, secretive, country we might say the conspiracies which *are* the state – or by the supranational bodies such as the European Union and the transnational corporations and their fronts. The UFO-alien-abduction frenzy of the 1990s is perhaps the most fascinating puzzle in the entire field this essay has surveyed but, when Tony Blair won his first election in 1997, four of his first cabinet were members of another Anglo-American network, the British-American Project, about which the media knew and had said nothing. Despite the publicity generated by the revelations of a string of former intelligence officers (Peter Wright, Colin Wallace and Cathy Massiter in the 1980s and former MI5 officers David Shayler and Annie Machon and former MI6 officer Richard Tomlinson more recently) the secret organisations of the British state remain unchallenged, unaccountable to the politicians and the electorate. I suspect that the powers-that-be would be very happy if we concentrated on alien abductions rather than – say – the parapolitical connections of the Blair faction in the Labour Party. All the baloney about all-encompassing conspiracies – from Jewish bankers to shape-shifting reptiles in the Windsor Castle – is simply a distraction.

Notes

1. Thus American columnist Alexander Cockburn:

   'To this day one can meet progressive types who devote many of their waking hours to activities designed to save Mumia abu Jamal who didn't give a toss about the Branch Davidians and their terrible slaughter by the federal government, and who still don't. Use the word "cult" and both reason and moral judgement enter recess.'

   From 'Waco and the Press' in *CounterPunch*, (USA) September 8, 1999.

2. The best single volume on the Kennedy assassination remains Anthony Summers' *The Kennedy Conspiracy*, the latest edition of which is from Warner Books, London, 1998. This is the place to start.

3. I do not know of any book-length study of this but see Carl Bernstein, 'The CIA and the Media' in *Rolling Stone,* 20 October 1977.

4. At <www.icdc.com/~paulwolf/cointelpro/churchfinalreportIIIa.htm> is the Church Committee's account of Cointelpro. More generally on the FBI's role in attacking the American left see Athan Theoharis and John Cox, *The Boss: J. Edgar Hoover and the Great American Inquisition* (London: Harrap, 1989).

The website <www.crunch.com/01> lists thousands of declassified FBI files.

5. From Wilson's introduction to Donald Holmes, *The Illuminati Conspiracy - The Sapien System*, (New Falcon Publication, 655 East Thunderbird Phoenix, AZ 85022).

6. This writer believes that some fairly recent evidence shows that the murder of JFK was organised by Vice President Johnson's entourage to head-off corruption inquiries into his activities. See Robin Ramsay, *Who Shot JFK?* in this Pocket Essentials series.

7. I am talking here as though Oswald was one person but there is considerable evidence that there were two 'Oswalds'. The most thorough account of this John Armstrong's 1000 page *Harvey and Lee* (Arlington, Texas: Quasar, 2003) which, although with all the faults of self-publication, is a fascinating piece of work. Various early – and much shorter – versions of this can be found on the Net searching for 'John Armstrong + Oswald'.

8. See William F. Pepper, *Orders to Kill: the truth behind the murder of Martin Luther King*, (New York: Carroll and Graf, 1995) or the update *An Act of State* (London: Verso, 2003). In December 1999 Pepper and the King family finally got to put their case for a conspiracy to the test in a civil suit. The jury found that King was murdered by a conspiracy. The AP report of the story is at <www.washingtonpost.com/wp-srv/aponline/ 19991208/ aponline182559_000.htm> An account of this trial is *An Act of State*.

9. On the RFK assassination and the role of Cesar see Dan Moldea, *The Killing of Robert F. Kennedy,* (London: W.W. Norton, 1995). After making an unanswerable case for a conspiracy in the first four-fifths of the book, in the final section Moldea tracks down Cesar and concludes, solely on the basis of a polygraph test, that Cesar is innocent and all the eyewitnesses and forensic evidence should be ignored.

   Polygraph testing is of dubious scientific value. Detailed information about polygraphy and the trickery on which it depends is available online at <www.nopolygraph.com>

   See also David T. Lykken's book, *A Tremor in the Blood: Uses and Abuses of the Lie Detector* (Plenum Press, 1998). This book provides a thorough debunking of polygraphy. Chapter 15 can be read online at <www.nopolygraph.com/chapter.htm>

10. This is not to suggest that pre-1963 there were *no* radical critics, *no* left, *no* investigative journalism – I. F. Stone, for one, comes to mind – but that there were not very many.

11. Vialls died in July 2005. I cannot imagine why the State Department thought him worthy of the honour of being the only named conspiracy theorist to be avoided. Ten years ago Vialls and I were talking because of a mutual interest in mind control. He told me of what he thought was a mind control project aimed at him which led him – not the Libyans – to shoot WPC Yvonne Fletcher from an office of the Hughes Tool Company. Mind-controlled assassin confesses? Yes, I

published this in *Lobster*, the magazine I edit. Vialls was not happy with this. Eventually he took a recognisable path, moving from areas in which he had expertise to elaborate fantasies and speculation across large areas of geopolitics.

12. A structural engineer explains why the Twin Towers fell the way they did – looking like a controlled demolition – at <www.pbs.org/wgbh/nova/wtc/collapse.html>.

13. There are two main theories: that the US government or state – at some unspecified level – organised the event; or that the US government/state let it happen. I do not believe the US government/state organised this, if only because (a) to do so would require co-operation between different US bureaucracies which is impossible to achieve and (b) the plan would involve too many people for it to be kept secret. When I wrote about 9/11 nine months after the event, I concluded that it was possible that the US government/state, having received many warnings about possible al-Qaeda threats, including plane hijacking plans, decided to let the attack happen to give itself the pretext for the attack on Afghanistan it was then planning. It was then caught out when the attacks turned out to be bigger than expected. How else to explain the total failure of the American air defence system that day?

On the 9/11 sceptics's claims see Ian Henshall and Rowland Morgan, *9.11 Revealed: Challenging the facts behind the War on Terror* (London: Robinson, 2005).

14. Quite why Moore attracted this is unclear. His film did

not contain a conspiracy theory, as far as I could see, merely hinted that perhaps the invasion of Iraq had something to do with the US government's relationship with the Saudis.

15. <http://ominous-valve.com/pac/archive/solomon.html>

16. <http://publiceye.org/conspire/conspiracism-911.html>

17. The process of being thus marginalised was described by Robert Parry. Working as a journalist for Associated Press in the 1980s, he began uncovering what became known as Iran-Contra and was rubbished by colleagues and political opponents in the Reagan administration as a 'conspiracy theorist'.

'Anorak' and 'train spotter' are concepts used and popularised in recent years by journalists to denigrate people with longer attention spans than their own. Many journalists' idea of research is nipping down to the cuttings library and having a quick squint, making a couple of phone calls to someone half a step ahead of themselves, or phoning some press officer for the departmental line. Most of them work on stories for hours rather than days, let alone weeks or years. A part of them knows this is not good enough and they fend off this uncomfortable thought by dismissing those with deeper or longer interests as anoraks, obsessives, hobbyists, and, the really useful one, 'people with an agenda'. Journalists are intensely suspicious of people 'with agendas' – even if, perhaps *especially* if – that agenda is a desire to get at the truth about something.

The accusation of 'conspiracy theorising' is also a useful way of providing a dismissive context for some potentially damaging evidence. A classic example of this was sent to me by Anthony Frewin. In an essay in the *Scientific American* (May 1999) Peta Firth discussed the controversy over bioengineering. This section appeared in the second paragraph of her piece.

'Conspiracy theories abounded — namely, that President Bill Clinton had personally pressured Prime Minister Tony Blair to give biotechnology companies, including Monsanto, a freer rein in planting GM crops. An admission on March 1 from John Prescott, Secretary of State for Environment, Transport and the Regions — that the British government had indeed received representations from its US counterpart about GM crops — did not help.'

Index

POCKET ESSENTIALS STOCK TITLES

1903047528	Alchemy & Alchemists Sean Martin 3.99
1903047722	American Civil War Phil Davies 3.99
1903047730	American Indian Wars Howard Hughes 3.99
1903047757	Ancient Greece Mike Paine 3.99
1903047854	The Beat Generation Jamie Russell 3.99
1903047919	Bisexuality Angie Bowie 3.99
1903047749	Black Death Sean Martin 3.99
1904048978	Bruce Springsteen 4.99
1904048099	Creative Writing Neil Nixon 3.99
1903047536	The Crusades Mike Paine 3.99 (R/P)
1904048277	Do Your Own PR Richard Milton 3.99
190304751X	Feminism Susan Osborne 3.99
1904048080	Film Studies Andrew M Butler 4.99
190304748X	Filming on a Microbudget NE Paul Hardy 4.99
1903047544	Freud & Psychoanalysis Nick Rennison 3.99
1904048218	Georges Simenon David Carter 3.99
1904048161	Globalisation Steven P McGiffen 3.99
1903047994	History of Witchcraft Lois Martin 3.99
1903047692	Jack the Ripper Whitehead/Rivett 3.99
1904048188	Jethro Tull Raymond Benson 3.99
1904048285	The Knights Templar Sean Martin 9.99 hb
1903047609	Laurel & Hardy Brian J Robb 3.99
1903047803	The Madchester Scene Richard Luck 3.99
1903047498	Nietzsche Travis Elborough 3.99
1903047110	Noir Fiction Paul Duncan 3.99
1904048226	Nuclear Paranoia C Newkey-Burden 3.99
1903047293	Philip K Dick Andrew M Butler 3.99
1904048242	Postmodernism Andrew M Butler 3.99
1903047838	The Rise of New Labour Robin Ramsay 3.99
1903047684	Sherlock Holmes Mark Campbell 3.99
1903047331	Stock Market Essentials Victor Cuadra 3.99
1904048064	Succeed in Music Business Paul Charles 3.99
1903047390	Terry Pratchett Andrew M Butler 3.99
1903047889	UFOs Neil Nixon 3.99
1904048250	The Universe Richard Osborne 9.99 hb
1904048358	Urban Legends 4.99
1904048129	Who Shot JFK? Robin Ramsay 3.99
1903047471	Writing a Screenplay John Costello 4.99

Or browse all our titles at www.pocketessentials.com

Available from all good bookshops or send a cheque to: Pocket Essentials (Dept SS), P.O. Box 394, Harpenden, Herts, AL5 1XJ. Please make cheques payable to 'Oldcastle Books', add 50p for postage and packing for each book in the UK and £1 elsewhere.

US customers can send $8.95 plus $1.95 postage and packing for each book payable to; Trafalgar Square Publishing, PO Box 257, Howe Hill, North Pomfret, Vermont 05053, USA email tsquare@sover.net

Customers worldwide can order online at www.pocketessentials.com